C-4807

MW00654711

THIS IS YOUR **PASSBOOK**® FOR ...

WASTEWATER TREATMENT ELECTRICIAN

N L C®

NATIONAL LEARNING CORPORATION®

passbooks.com

COPYRIGHT NOTICE

Copyright © 2020 by

National Learning Corporation

212 Michael Drive, Syosset, NY 11791
(516) 921-8888 • www.passbooks.com
E-mail: info@passbooks.com

PUBLISHED IN THE UNITED STATES OF AMERICA

PASSBOOK® SERIES

THE *PASSBOOK® SERIES* has been created to prepare applicants and candidates for the ultimate academic battlefield – the examination room.

At some time in our lives, each and every one of us may be required to take an examination – for validation, matriculation, admission, qualification, registration, certification, or licensure.

Based on the assumption that every applicant or candidate has met the basic formal educational standards, has taken the required number of courses, and read the necessary texts, the *PASSBOOK® SERIES* furnishes the one special preparation which may assure passing with confidence, instead of failing with insecurity. Examination questions – together with answers – are furnished as the basic vehicle for study so that the mysteries of the examination and its compounding difficulties may be eliminated or diminished by a sure method.

This book is meant to help you pass your examination provided that you qualify and are serious in your objective.

The entire field is reviewed through the huge store of content information which is succinctly presented through a provocative and challenging approach – the question-and-answer method.

A climate of success is established by furnishing the correct answers at the end of each test.

You soon learn to recognize types of questions, forms of questions, and patterns of questioning. You may even begin to anticipate expected outcomes.

You perceive that many questions are repeated or adapted so that you can gain acute insights, which may enable you to score many sure points.

You learn how to confront new questions, or types of questions, and to attack them confidently and work out the correct answers.

You note objectives and emphases, and recognize pitfalls and dangers, so that you may make positive educational adjustments.

Moreover, you are kept fully informed in relation to new concepts, methods, practices, and directions in the field.

You discover that you arre actually taking the examination all the time: you are preparing for the examination by "taking" an examination, not by reading extraneous and/or supererogatory textbooks.

In short, this PASSBOOK®, used directedly, should be an important factor in helping you to pass your test.

WASTEWATER TREATMENT ELECTRICIAN

DUTIES:

A Wastewater Treatment Electrician performs skilled electrical work in the installation, maintenance, overhaul, repair, and testing of power generating and distribution equipment, rotating equipment and their associated digital and analog controls including micro-processor based controls, devices and systems; utility protective relays and controls; fiber optic cable, terminations and devices; communications and signaling systems; standby and emergency power sources, and other electrical equipment found in wastewater collection and treatment facilities; and may serve as a lead worker for other employees engaged in this work.

SCOPE OF THE EXAMINATION:

The examination will consist of a multiple-choice written test in which candidates may be examined for knowledge of: different types of installations such as industrial, process, office and underground; theory and principles of direct current and alternating current; safety principles, regulations, practices and procedures for working near energize equipment or areas of high fire danger, and protective clothing and equipment; mathematics sufficient to calculate lengths, areas, volumes, and quantities of materials and to do electrical calculations such as power factors, current-voltage relationships, or setting ranges on meters; ability to: construct electrical systems; use and modify plans for electrical construction in compliance with the Codes and safety orders; install, inspect, maintain, overhaul, repair, and troubleshoot low, medium, and high voltage transformers, meter and conventional controls, relays, protective devices, and power consumption meters, 110v and 220v wiring and lighting systems, low, medium, and high voltage switchboards and switching systems, motors and generators, motor control systems, uninterruptible power supplies, and batteries and D. power supplies; read and interpret technical reports, diagrams, codes; and other necessary skills, knowledge and abilities.

HOW TO TAKE A TEST

I. YOU MUST PASS AN EXAMINATION

A. *WHAT EVERY CANDIDATE SHOULD KNOW*

Examination applicants often ask us for help in preparing for the written test. What can I study in advance? What kinds of questions will be asked? How will the test be given? How will the papers be graded?

As an applicant for a civil service examination, you may be wondering about some of these things. Our purpose here is to suggest effective methods of advance study and to describe civil service examinations.

Your chances for success on this examination can be increased if you know how to prepare. Those "pre-examination jitters" can be reduced if you know what to expect. You can even experience an adventure in good citizenship if you know why civil service exams are given.

B. *WHY ARE CIVIL SERVICE EXAMINATIONS GIVEN?*

Civil service examinations are important to you in two ways. As a citizen, you want public jobs filled by employees who know how to do their work. As a job seeker, you want a fair chance to compete for that job on an equal footing with other candidates. The best-known means of accomplishing this two-fold goal is the competitive examination.

Exams are widely publicized throughout the nation. They may be administered for jobs in federal, state, city, municipal, town or village governments or agencies.

Any citizen may apply, with some limitations, such as the age or residence of applicants. Your experience and education may be reviewed to see whether you meet the requirements for the particular examination. When these requirements exist, they are reasonable and applied consistently to all applicants. Thus, a competitive examination may cause you some uneasiness now, but it is your privilege and safeguard.

C. *HOW ARE CIVIL SERVICE EXAMS DEVELOPED?*

Examinations are carefully written by trained technicians who are specialists in the field known as "psychological measurement," in consultation with recognized authorities in the field of work that the test will cover. These experts recommend the subject matter areas or skills to be tested; only those knowledges or skills important to your success on the job are included. The most reliable books and source materials available are used as references. Together, the experts and technicians judge the difficulty level of the questions.

Test technicians know how to phrase questions so that the problem is clearly stated. Their ethics do not permit "trick" or "catch" questions. Questions may have been tried out on sample groups, or subjected to statistical analysis, to determine their usefulness.

Written tests are often used in combination with performance tests, ratings of training and experience, and oral interviews. All of these measures combine to form the best-known means of finding the right person for the right job.

II. HOW TO PASS THE WRITTEN TEST

A. NATURE OF THE EXAMINATION

To prepare intelligently for civil service examinations, you should know how they differ from school examinations you have taken. In school you were assigned certain definite pages to read or subjects to cover. The examination questions were quite detailed and usually emphasized memory. Civil service exams, on the other hand, try to discover your present ability to perform the duties of a position, plus your potentiality to learn these duties. In other words, a civil service exam attempts to predict how successful you will be. Questions cover such a broad area that they cannot be as minute and detailed as school exam questions.

In the public service similar kinds of work, or positions, are grouped together in one "class." This process is known as *position-classification*. All the positions in a class are paid according to the salary range for that class. One class title covers all of these positions, and they are all tested by the same examination.

B. FOUR BASIC STEPS

1) Study the announcement

How, then, can you know what subjects to study? Our best answer is: "Learn as much as possible about the class of positions for which you've applied." The exam will test the knowledge, skills and abilities needed to do the work.

Your most valuable source of information about the position you want is the official exam announcement. This announcement lists the training and experience qualifications. Check these standards and apply only if you come reasonably close to meeting them.

The brief description of the position in the examination announcement offers some clues to the subjects which will be tested. Think about the job itself. Review the duties in your mind. Can you perform them, or are there some in which you are rusty? Fill in the blank spots in your preparation.

Many jurisdictions preview the written test in the exam announcement by including a section called "Knowledge and Abilities Required," "Scope of the Examination," or some similar heading. Here you will find out specifically what fields will be tested.

2) Review your own background

Once you learn in general what the position is all about, and what you need to know to do the work, ask yourself which subjects you already know fairly well and which need improvement. You may wonder whether to concentrate on improving your strong areas or on building some background in your fields of weakness. When the announcement has specified "some knowledge" or "considerable knowledge," or has used adjectives like "beginning principles of…" or "advanced … methods," you can get a clue as to the number and difficulty of questions to be asked in any given field. More questions, and hence broader coverage, would be included for those subjects which are more important in the work. Now weigh your strengths and weaknesses against the job requirements and prepare accordingly.

3) Determine the level of the position

Another way to tell how intensively you should prepare is to understand the level of the job for which you are applying. Is it the entering level? In other words, is this the position in which beginners in a field of work are hired? Or is it an intermediate or advanced level? Sometimes this is indicated by such words as "Junior" or "Senior" in the class title. Other jurisdictions use Roman numerals to designate the level – Clerk I, Clerk II, for example. The word "Supervisor" sometimes appears in the title. If the level is not indicated by the title, check the description of duties. Will you be working under very close supervision, or will you have responsibility for independent decisions in this work?

4) Choose appropriate study materials

Now that you know the subjects to be examined and the relative amount of each subject to be covered, you can choose suitable study materials. For beginning level jobs, or even advanced ones, if you have a pronounced weakness in some aspect of your training, read a modern, standard textbook in that field. Be sure it is up to date and has general coverage. Such books are normally available at your library, and the librarian will be glad to help you locate one. For entry-level positions, questions of appropriate difficulty are chosen – neither highly advanced questions, nor those too simple. Such questions require careful thought but not advanced training.

If the position for which you are applying is technical or advanced, you will read more advanced, specialized material. If you are already familiar with the basic principles of your field, elementary textbooks would waste your time. Concentrate on advanced textbooks and technical periodicals. Think through the concepts and review difficult problems in your field.

These are all general sources. You can get more ideas on your own initiative, following these leads. For example, training manuals and publications of the government agency which employs workers in your field can be useful, particularly for technical and professional positions. A letter or visit to the government department involved may result in more specific study suggestions, and certainly will provide you with a more definite idea of the exact nature of the position you are seeking.

III. KINDS OF TESTS

Tests are used for purposes other than measuring knowledge and ability to perform specified duties. For some positions, it is equally important to test ability to make adjustments to new situations or to profit from training. In others, basic mental abilities not dependent on information are essential. Questions which test these things may not appear as pertinent to the duties of the position as those which test for knowledge and information. Yet they are often highly important parts of a fair examination. For very general questions, it is almost impossible to help you direct your study efforts. What we can do is to point out some of the more common of these general abilities needed in public service positions and describe some typical questions.

1) General information

Broad, general information has been found useful for predicting job success in some kinds of work. This is tested in a variety of ways, from vocabulary lists to questions about current events. Basic background in some field of work, such as sociology or economics, may be sampled in a group of questions. Often these are principles which have become familiar to most persons through exposure rather than through formal training. It is difficult to advise you how to study for these questions; being alert to the world around you is our best suggestion.

2) Verbal ability

An example of an ability needed in many positions is verbal or language ability. Verbal ability is, in brief, the ability to use and understand words. Vocabulary and grammar tests are typical measures of this ability. Reading comprehension or paragraph interpretation questions are common in many kinds of civil service tests. You are given a paragraph of written material and asked to find its central meaning.

3) Numerical ability

Number skills can be tested by the familiar arithmetic problem, by checking paired lists of numbers to see which are alike and which are different, or by interpreting charts and graphs. In the latter test, a graph may be printed in the test booklet which you are asked to use as the basis for answering questions.

4) Observation

A popular test for law-enforcement positions is the observation test. A picture is shown to you for several minutes, then taken away. Questions about the picture test your ability to observe both details and larger elements.

5) Following directions

In many positions in the public service, the employee must be able to carry out written instructions dependably and accurately. You may be given a chart with several columns, each column listing a variety of information. The questions require you to carry out directions involving the information given in the chart.

6) Skills and aptitudes

Performance tests effectively measure some manual skills and aptitudes. When the skill is one in which you are trained, such as typing or shorthand, you can practice. These tests are often very much like those given in business school or high school courses. For many of the other skills and aptitudes, however, no short-time preparation can be made. Skills and abilities natural to you or that you have developed throughout your lifetime are being tested.

Many of the general questions just described provide all the data needed to answer the questions and ask you to use your reasoning ability to find the answers. Your best preparation for these tests, as well as for tests of facts and ideas, is to be at your physical and mental best. You, no doubt, have your own methods of getting into an exam-taking mood and keeping "in shape." The next section lists some ideas on this subject.

IV. KINDS OF QUESTIONS

Only rarely is the "essay" question, which you answer in narrative form, used in civil service tests. Civil service tests are usually of the short-answer type. Full instructions for answering these questions will be given to you at the examination. But in case this is your first experience with short-answer questions and separate answer sheets, here is what you need to know:

1) Multiple-choice Questions

Most popular of the short-answer questions is the "multiple choice" or "best answer" question. It can be used, for example, to test for factual knowledge, ability to solve problems or judgment in meeting situations found at work.

A multiple-choice question is normally one of three types—

- It can begin with an incomplete statement followed by several possible endings. You are to find the one ending which *best* completes the statement, although some of the others may not be entirely wrong.
- It can also be a complete statement in the form of a question which is answered by choosing one of the statements listed.
- It can be in the form of a problem – again you select the best answer.

Here is an example of a multiple-choice question with a discussion which should give you some clues as to the method for choosing the right answer:

When an employee has a complaint about his assignment, the action which will *best* help him overcome his difficulty is to
A. discuss his difficulty with his coworkers
B. take the problem to the head of the organization
C. take the problem to the person who gave him the assignment
D. say nothing to anyone about his complaint

In answering this question, you should study each of the choices to find which is best. Consider choice "A" – Certainly an employee may discuss his complaint with fellow employees, but no change or improvement can result, and the complaint remains unresolved. Choice "B" is a poor choice since the head of the organization probably does not know what assignment you have been given, and taking your problem to him is known as "going over the head" of the supervisor. The supervisor, or person who made the assignment, is the person who can clarify it or correct any injustice. Choice "C" is, therefore, correct. To say nothing, as in choice "D," is unwise. Supervisors have and interest in knowing the problems employees are facing, and the employee is seeking a solution to his problem.

2) True/False Questions

The "true/false" or "right/wrong" form of question is sometimes used. Here a complete statement is given. Your job is to decide whether the statement is right or wrong.

SAMPLE: A roaming cell-phone call to a nearby city costs less than a non-roaming call to a distant city.

This statement is wrong, or false, since roaming calls are more expensive.
This is not a complete list of all possible question forms, although most of the others are variations of these common types. You will always get complete directions for

answering questions. Be sure you understand *how* to mark your answers – ask questions until you do.

V. RECORDING YOUR ANSWERS

Computer terminals are used more and more today for many different kinds of exams.

For an examination with very few applicants, you may be told to record your answers in the test booklet itself. Separate answer sheets are much more common. If this separate answer sheet is to be scored by machine – and this is often the case – it is highly important that you mark your answers correctly in order to get credit.

An electronic scoring machine is often used in civil service offices because of the speed with which papers can be scored. Machine-scored answer sheets must be marked with a pencil, which will be given to you. This pencil has a high graphite content which responds to the electronic scoring machine. As a matter of fact, stray dots may register as answers, so do not let your pencil rest on the answer sheet while you are pondering the correct answer. Also, if your pencil lead breaks or is otherwise defective, ask for another.

Since the answer sheet will be dropped in a slot in the scoring machine, be careful not to bend the corners or get the paper crumpled.

The answer sheet normally has five vertical columns of numbers, with 30 numbers to a column. These numbers correspond to the question numbers in your test booklet. After each number, going across the page are four or five pairs of dotted lines. These short dotted lines have small letters or numbers above them. The first two pairs may also have a "T" or "F" above the letters. This indicates that the first two pairs only are to be used if the questions are of the true-false type. If the questions are multiple choice, disregard the "T" and "F" and pay attention only to the small letters or numbers.

Answer your questions in the manner of the sample that follows:

32. The largest city in the United States is
    A. Washington, D.C.
    B. New York City
    C. Chicago
    D. Detroit
    E. San Francisco

1) Choose the answer you think is best. (New York City is the largest, so "B" is correct.)
2) Find the row of dotted lines numbered the same as the question you are answering. (Find row number 32)
3) Find the pair of dotted lines corresponding to the answer. (Find the pair of lines under the mark "B.")
4) Make a solid black mark between the dotted lines.

VI. BEFORE THE TEST

Common sense will help you find procedures to follow to get ready for an examination. Too many of us, however, overlook these sensible measures. Indeed, nervousness and fatigue have been found to be the most serious reasons why applicants fail to do their best on civil service tests. Here is a list of reminders:

- Begin your preparation early – Don't wait until the last minute to go scurrying around for books and materials or to find out what the position is all about.
- Prepare continuously – An hour a night for a week is better than an all-night cram session. This has been definitely established. What is more, a night a week for a month will return better dividends than crowding your study into a shorter period of time.
- Locate the place of the exam – You have been sent a notice telling you when and where to report for the examination. If the location is in a different town or otherwise unfamiliar to you, it would be well to inquire the best route and learn something about the building.
- Relax the night before the test – Allow your mind to rest. Do not study at all that night. Plan some mild recreation or diversion; then go to bed early and get a good night's sleep.
- Get up early enough to make a leisurely trip to the place for the test – This way unforeseen events, traffic snarls, unfamiliar buildings, etc. will not upset you.
- Dress comfortably – A written test is not a fashion show. You will be known by number and not by name, so wear something comfortable.
- Leave excess paraphernalia at home – Shopping bags and odd bundles will get in your way. You need bring only the items mentioned in the official notice you received; usually everything you need is provided. Do not bring reference books to the exam. They will only confuse those last minutes and be taken away from you when in the test room.
- Arrive somewhat ahead of time – If because of transportation schedules you must get there very early, bring a newspaper or magazine to take your mind off yourself while waiting.
- Locate the examination room – When you have found the proper room, you will be directed to the seat or part of the room where you will sit. Sometimes you are given a sheet of instructions to read while you are waiting. Do not fill out any forms until you are told to do so; just read them and be prepared.
- Relax and prepare to listen to the instructions
- If you have any physical problem that may keep you from doing your best, be sure to tell the test administrator. If you are sick or in poor health, you really cannot do your best on the exam. You can come back and take the test some other time.

VII. AT THE TEST

The day of the test is here and you have the test booklet in your hand. The temptation to get going is very strong. Caution! There is more to success than knowing the right answers. You must know how to identify your papers and understand variations in the type of short-answer question used in this particular examination. Follow these suggestions for maximum results from your efforts:

1) Cooperate with the monitor

The test administrator has a duty to create a situation in which you can be as much at ease as possible. He will give instructions, tell you when to begin, check to see that you are marking your answer sheet correctly, and so on. He is not there to guard you, although he will see that your competitors do not take unfair advantage. He wants to help you do your best.

2) Listen to all instructions

Don't jump the gun! Wait until you understand all directions. In most civil service tests you get more time than you need to answer the questions. So don't be in a hurry. Read each word of instructions until you clearly understand the meaning. Study the examples, listen to all announcements and follow directions. Ask questions if you do not understand what to do.

3) Identify your papers

Civil service exams are usually identified by number only. You will be assigned a number; you must not put your name on your test papers. Be sure to copy your number correctly. Since more than one exam may be given, copy your exact examination title.

4) Plan your time

Unless you are told that a test is a "speed" or "rate of work" test, speed itself is usually not important. Time enough to answer all the questions will be provided, but this does not mean that you have all day. An overall time limit has been set. Divide the total time (in minutes) by the number of questions to determine the approximate time you have for each question.

5) Do not linger over difficult questions

If you come across a difficult question, mark it with a paper clip (useful to have along) and come back to it when you have been through the booklet. One caution if you do this – be sure to skip a number on your answer sheet as well. Check often to be sure that you have not lost your place and that you are marking in the row numbered the same as the question you are answering.

6) Read the questions

Be sure you know what the question asks! Many capable people are unsuccessful because they failed to *read* the questions correctly.

7) Answer all questions

Unless you have been instructed that a penalty will be deducted for incorrect answers, it is better to guess than to omit a question.

8) Speed tests

It is often better NOT to guess on speed tests. It has been found that on timed tests people are tempted to spend the last few seconds before time is called in marking answers at random – without even reading them – in the hope of picking up a few extra points. To discourage this practice, the instructions may warn you that your score will be "corrected" for guessing. That is, a penalty will be applied. The incorrect answers will be deducted from the correct ones, or some other penalty formula will be used.

9) Review your answers

If you finish before time is called, go back to the questions you guessed or omitted to give them further thought. Review other answers if you have time.

10) Return your test materials

If you are ready to leave before others have finished or time is called, take ALL your materials to the monitor and leave quietly. Never take any test material with you. The monitor can discover whose papers are not complete, and taking a test booklet may be grounds for disqualification.

VIII. EXAMINATION TECHNIQUES

1) Read the general instructions carefully. These are usually printed on the first page of the exam booklet. As a rule, these instructions refer to the timing of the examination; the fact that you should not start work until the signal and must stop work at a signal, etc. If there are any *special* instructions, such as a choice of questions to be answered, make sure that you note this instruction carefully.

2) When you are ready to start work on the examination, that is as soon as the signal has been given, read the instructions to each question booklet, underline any key words or phrases, such as *least, best, outline, describe* and the like. In this way you will tend to answer as requested rather than discover on reviewing your paper that you *listed without describing*, that you selected the *worst* choice rather than the *best* choice, etc.

3) If the examination is of the objective or multiple-choice type – that is, each question will also give a series of possible answers: A, B, C or D, and you are called upon to select the best answer and write the letter next to that answer on your answer paper – it is advisable to start answering each question in turn. There may be anywhere from 50 to 100 such questions in the three or four hours allotted and you can see how much time would be taken if you read through all the questions before beginning to answer any. Furthermore, if you come across a question or group of questions which you know would be difficult to answer, it would undoubtedly affect your handling of all the other questions.

4) If the examination is of the essay type and contains but a few questions, it is a moot point as to whether you should read all the questions before starting to answer any one. Of course, if you are given a choice – say five out of seven and the like – then it is essential to read all the questions so you can eliminate the two that are most difficult. If, however, you are asked to answer all the questions, there may be danger in trying to answer the easiest one first because you may find that you will spend too much time on it. The best technique is to answer the first question, then proceed to the second, etc.

5) Time your answers. Before the exam begins, write down the time it started, then add the time allowed for the examination and write down the time it must be completed, then divide the time available somewhat as follows:

- If 3-1/2 hours are allowed, that would be 210 minutes. If you have 80 objective-type questions, that would be an average of 2-1/2 minutes per question. Allow yourself no more than 2 minutes per question, or a total of 160 minutes, which will permit about 50 minutes to review.
- If for the time allotment of 210 minutes there are 7 essay questions to answer, that would average about 30 minutes a question. Give yourself only 25 minutes per question so that you have about 35 minutes to review.

6) The most important instruction is to *read each question* and make sure you know what is wanted. The second most important instruction is to *time yourself properly* so that you answer every question. The third most important instruction is to *answer every question*. Guess if you have to but include something for each question. Remember that you will receive no credit for a blank and will probably receive some credit if you write something in answer to an essay question. If you guess a letter – say "B" for a multiple-choice question – you may have guessed right. If you leave a blank as an answer to a multiple-choice question, the examiners may respect your feelings but it will not add a point to your score. Some exams may penalize you for wrong answers, so in such cases *only*, you may not want to guess unless you have some basis for your answer.

7) Suggestions
   a. Objective-type questions
      1. Examine the question booklet for proper sequence of pages and questions
      2. Read all instructions carefully
      3. Skip any question which seems too difficult; return to it after all other questions have been answered
      4. Apportion your time properly; do not spend too much time on any single question or group of questions
      5. Note and underline key words – *all, most, fewest, least, best, worst, same, opposite,* etc.
      6. Pay particular attention to negatives
      7. Note unusual option, e.g., unduly long, short, complex, different or similar in content to the body of the question
      8. Observe the use of "hedging" words – *probably, may, most likely,* etc.
      9. Make sure that your answer is put next to the same number as the question
      10. Do not second-guess unless you have good reason to believe the second answer is definitely more correct
      11. Cross out original answer if you decide another answer is more accurate; do not erase until you are ready to hand your paper in
      12. Answer all questions; guess unless instructed otherwise
      13. Leave time for review

   b. Essay questions
      1. Read each question carefully
      2. Determine exactly what is wanted. Underline key words or phrases.
      3. Decide on outline or paragraph answer

4. Include many different points and elements unless asked to develop any one or two points or elements
5. Show impartiality by giving pros and cons unless directed to select one side only
6. Make and write down any assumptions you find necessary to answer the questions
7. Watch your English, grammar, punctuation and choice of words
8. Time your answers; don't crowd material

8) Answering the essay question

Most essay questions can be answered by framing the specific response around several key words or ideas. Here are a few such key words or ideas:

M's: manpower, materials, methods, money, management
P's: purpose, program, policy, plan, procedure, practice, problems, pitfalls, personnel, public relations
  a. Six basic steps in handling problems:
    1. Preliminary plan and background development
    2. Collect information, data and facts
    3. Analyze and interpret information, data and facts
    4. Analyze and develop solutions as well as make recommendations
    5. Prepare report and sell recommendations
    6. Install recommendations and follow up effectiveness

  b. Pitfalls to avoid
    1. *Taking things for granted* – A statement of the situation does not necessarily imply that each of the elements is necessarily true; for example, a complaint may be invalid and biased so that all that can be taken for granted is that a complaint has been registered
    2. *Considering only one side of a situation* – Wherever possible, indicate several alternatives and then point out the reasons you selected the best one
    3. *Failing to indicate follow up* – Whenever your answer indicates action on your part, make certain that you will take proper follow-up action to see how successful your recommendations, procedures or actions turn out to be
    4. *Taking too long in answering any single question* – Remember to time your answers properly

IX. AFTER THE TEST

Scoring procedures differ in detail among civil service jurisdictions although the general principles are the same. Whether the papers are hand-scored or graded by machine we have described, they are nearly always graded by number. That is, the person who marks the paper knows only the number – never the name – of the applicant. Not until all the papers have been graded will they be matched with names. If other tests, such as training and experience or oral interview ratings have been given, scores will be combined. Different parts of the examination usually have different weights. For example, the written test might count 60 percent of the final grade, and a rating of training and experience 40 percent. In many jurisdictions, veterans will have a certain number of points added to their grades.

After the final grade has been determined, the names are placed in grade order and an eligible list is established. There are various methods for resolving ties between those who get the same final grade – probably the most common is to place first the name of the person whose application was received first. Job offers are made from the eligible list in the order the names appear on it. You will be notified of your grade and your rank as soon as all these computations have been made. This will be done as rapidly as possible.

People who are found to meet the requirements in the announcement are called "eligibles." Their names are put on a list of eligible candidates. An eligible's chances of getting a job depend on how high he stands on this list and how fast agencies are filling jobs from the list.

When a job is to be filled from a list of eligibles, the agency asks for the names of people on the list of eligibles for that job. When the civil service commission receives this request, it sends to the agency the names of the three people highest on this list. Or, if the job to be filled has specialized requirements, the office sends the agency the names of the top three persons who meet these requirements from the general list.

The appointing officer makes a choice from among the three people whose names were sent to him. If the selected person accepts the appointment, the names of the others are put back on the list to be considered for future openings.

That is the rule in hiring from all kinds of eligible lists, whether they are for typist, carpenter, chemist, or something else. For every vacancy, the appointing officer has his choice of any one of the top three eligibles on the list. This explains why the person whose name is on top of the list sometimes does not get an appointment when some of the persons lower on the list do. If the appointing officer chooses the second or third eligible, the No. 1 eligible does not get a job at once, but stays on the list until he is appointed or the list is terminated.

X. HOW TO PASS THE INTERVIEW TEST

The examination for which you applied requires an oral interview test. You have already taken the written test and you are now being called for the interview test – the final part of the formal examination.

You may think that it is not possible to prepare for an interview test and that there are no procedures to follow during an interview. Our purpose is to point out some things you can do in advance that will help you and some good rules to follow and pitfalls to avoid while you are being interviewed.

What is an interview supposed to test?
The written examination is designed to test the technical knowledge and competence of the candidate; the oral is designed to evaluate intangible qualities, not readily measured otherwise, and to establish a list showing the relative fitness of each candidate – as measured against his competitors – for the position sought. Scoring is not on the basis of "right" and "wrong," but on a sliding scale of values ranging from "not passable" to "outstanding." As a matter of fact, it is possible to achieve a relatively low score without a single "incorrect" answer because of evident weakness in the qualities being measured.

Occasionally, an examination may consist entirely of an oral test – either an individual or a group oral. In such cases, information is sought concerning the technical knowledges and abilities of the candidate, since there has been no written examination for this purpose. More commonly, however, an oral test is used to supplement a written examination.

Who conducts interviews?

The composition of oral boards varies among different jurisdictions. In nearly all, a representative of the personnel department serves as chairman. One of the members of the board may be a representative of the department in which the candidate would work. In some cases, "outside experts" are used, and, frequently, a businessman or some other representative of the general public is asked to serve. Labor and management or other special groups may be represented. The aim is to secure the services of experts in the appropriate field.

However the board is composed, it is a good idea (and not at all improper or unethical) to ascertain in advance of the interview who the members are and what groups they represent. When you are introduced to them, you will have some idea of their backgrounds and interests, and at least you will not stutter and stammer over their names.

What should be done before the interview?

While knowledge about the board members is useful and takes some of the surprise element out of the interview, there is other preparation which is more substantive. It *is* possible to prepare for an oral interview – in several ways:

1) Keep a copy of your application and review it carefully before the interview

This may be the only document before the oral board, and the starting point of the interview. Know what education and experience you have listed there, and the sequence and dates of all of it. Sometimes the board will ask you to review the highlights of your experience for them; you should not have to hem and haw doing it.

2) Study the class specification and the examination announcement

Usually, the oral board has one or both of these to guide them. The qualities, characteristics or knowledges required by the position sought are stated in these documents. They offer valuable clues as to the nature of the oral interview. For example, if the job involves supervisory responsibilities, the announcement will usually indicate that knowledge of modern supervisory methods and the qualifications of the candidate as a supervisor will be tested. If so, you can expect such questions, frequently in the form of a hypothetical situation which you are expected to solve. NEVER go into an oral without knowledge of the duties and responsibilities of the job you seek.

3) Think through each qualification required

Try to visualize the kind of questions you would ask if you were a board member. How well could you answer them? Try especially to appraise your own knowledge and background in each area, *measured against the job sought*, and identify any areas in which you are weak. Be critical and realistic – do not flatter yourself.

4) Do some general reading in areas in which you feel you may be weak
For example, if the job involves supervision and your past experience has NOT, some general reading in supervisory methods and practices, particularly in the field of human relations, might be useful. Do NOT study agency procedures or detailed manuals. The oral board will be testing your understanding and capacity, not your memory.

5) Get a good night's sleep and watch your general health and mental attitude
You will want a clear head at the interview. Take care of a cold or any other minor ailment, and of course, no hangovers.

What should be done on the day of the interview?
Now comes the day of the interview itself. Give yourself plenty of time to get there. Plan to arrive somewhat ahead of the scheduled time, particularly if your appointment is in the fore part of the day. If a previous candidate fails to appear, the board might be ready for you a bit early. By early afternoon an oral board is almost invariably behind schedule if there are many candidates, and you may have to wait. Take along a book or magazine to read, or your application to review, but leave any extraneous material in the waiting room when you go in for your interview. In any event, relax and compose yourself.

The matter of dress is important. The board is forming impressions about you – from your experience, your manners, your attitude, and your appearance. Give your personal appearance careful attention. Dress your best, but not your flashiest. Choose conservative, appropriate clothing, and be sure it is immaculate. This is a business interview, and your appearance should indicate that you regard it as such. Besides, being well groomed and properly dressed will help boost your confidence.

Sooner or later, someone will call your name and escort you into the interview room. *This is it.* From here on you are on your own. It is too late for any more preparation. But remember, you asked for this opportunity to prove your fitness, and you are here because your request was granted.

What happens when you go in?
The usual sequence of events will be as follows: The clerk (who is often the board stenographer) will introduce you to the chairman of the oral board, who will introduce you to the other members of the board. Acknowledge the introductions before you sit down. Do not be surprised if you find a microphone facing you or a stenotypist sitting by. Oral interviews are usually recorded in the event of an appeal or other review.

Usually the chairman of the board will open the interview by reviewing the highlights of your education and work experience from your application – primarily for the benefit of the other members of the board, as well as to get the material into the record. Do not interrupt or comment unless there is an error or significant misinterpretation; if that is the case, do not hesitate. But do not quibble about insignificant matters. Also, he will usually ask you some question about your education, experience or your present job – partly to get you to start talking and to establish the interviewing "rapport." He may start the actual questioning, or turn it over to one of the other members. Frequently, each member undertakes the questioning on a particular area, one in which he is perhaps most competent, so you can expect each member to participate in the examination. Because time is limited, you may also expect some rather abrupt switches in the direction the questioning takes, so do not be upset by it. Normally, a board member will not pursue a single line of questioning unless he discovers a particular strength or weakness.

After each member has participated, the chairman will usually ask whether any member has any further questions, then will ask you if you have anything you wish to add. Unless you are expecting this question, it may floor you. Worse, it may start you off on an extended, extemporaneous speech. The board is not usually seeking more information. The question is principally to offer you a last opportunity to present further qualifications or to indicate that you have nothing to add. So, if you feel that a significant qualification or characteristic has been overlooked, it is proper to point it out in a sentence or so. Do not compliment the board on the thoroughness of their examination – they have been sketchy, and you know it. If you wish, merely say, "No thank you, I have nothing further to add." This is a point where you can "talk yourself out" of a good impression or fail to present an important bit of information. Remember, *you close the interview yourself.*

The chairman will then say, "That is all, Mr. _____, thank you." Do not be startled; the interview is over, and quicker than you think. Thank him, gather your belongings and take your leave. Save your sigh of relief for the other side of the door.

How to put your best foot forward

Throughout this entire process, you may feel that the board individually and collectively is trying to pierce your defenses, seek out your hidden weaknesses and embarrass and confuse you. Actually, this is not true. They are obliged to make an appraisal of your qualifications for the job you are seeking, and they want to see you in your best light. Remember, they must interview all candidates and a non-cooperative candidate may become a failure in spite of their best efforts to bring out his qualifications. Here are 15 suggestions that will help you:

1) Be natural – Keep your attitude confident, not cocky

If you are not confident that you can do the job, do not expect the board to be. Do not apologize for your weaknesses, try to bring out your strong points. The board is interested in a positive, not negative, presentation. Cockiness will antagonize any board member and make him wonder if you are covering up a weakness by a false show of strength.

2) Get comfortable, but don't lounge or sprawl

Sit erectly but not stiffly. A careless posture may lead the board to conclude that you are careless in other things, or at least that you are not impressed by the importance of the occasion. Either conclusion is natural, even if incorrect. Do not fuss with your clothing, a pencil or an ashtray. Your hands may occasionally be useful to emphasize a point; do not let them become a point of distraction.

3) Do not wisecrack or make small talk

This is a serious situation, and your attitude should show that you consider it as such. Further, the time of the board is limited – they do not want to waste it, and neither should you.

4) Do not exaggerate your experience or abilities

In the first place, from information in the application or other interviews and sources, the board may know more about you than you think. Secondly, you probably will not get away with it. An experienced board is rather adept at spotting such a situation, so do not take the chance.

5) If you know a board member, do not make a point of it, yet do not hide it

Certainly you are not fooling him, and probably not the other members of the board. Do not try to take advantage of your acquaintanceship – it will probably do you little good.

6) Do not dominate the interview

Let the board do that. They will give you the clues – do not assume that you have to do all the talking. Realize that the board has a number of questions to ask you, and do not try to take up all the interview time by showing off your extensive knowledge of the answer to the first one.

7) Be attentive

You only have 20 minutes or so, and you should keep your attention at its sharpest throughout. When a member is addressing a problem or question to you, give him your undivided attention. Address your reply principally to him, but do not exclude the other board members.

8) Do not interrupt

A board member may be stating a problem for you to analyze. He will ask you a question when the time comes. Let him state the problem, and wait for the question.

9) Make sure you understand the question

Do not try to answer until you are sure what the question is. If it is not clear, restate it in your own words or ask the board member to clarify it for you. However, do not haggle about minor elements.

10) Reply promptly but not hastily

A common entry on oral board rating sheets is "candidate responded readily," or "candidate hesitated in replies." Respond as promptly and quickly as you can, but do not jump to a hasty, ill-considered answer.

11) Do not be peremptory in your answers

A brief answer is proper – but do not fire your answer back. That is a losing game from your point of view. The board member can probably ask questions much faster than you can answer them.

12) Do not try to create the answer you think the board member wants

He is interested in what kind of mind you have and how it works – not in playing games. Furthermore, he can usually spot this practice and will actually grade you down on it.

13) Do not switch sides in your reply merely to agree with a board member

Frequently, a member will take a contrary position merely to draw you out and to see if you are willing and able to defend your point of view. Do not start a debate, yet do not surrender a good position. If a position is worth taking, it is worth defending.

14) Do not be afraid to admit an error in judgment if you are shown to be wrong

The board knows that you are forced to reply without any opportunity for careful consideration. Your answer may be demonstrably wrong. If so, admit it and get on with the interview.

15) Do not dwell at length on your present job

The opening question may relate to your present assignment. Answer the question but do not go into an extended discussion. You are being examined for a *new* job, not your present one. As a matter of fact, try to phrase ALL your answers in terms of the job for which you are being examined.

Basis of Rating

Probably you will forget most of these "do's" and "don'ts" when you walk into the oral interview room. Even remembering them all will not ensure you a passing grade. Perhaps you did not have the qualifications in the first place. But remembering them will help you to put your best foot forward, without treading on the toes of the board members.

Rumor and popular opinion to the contrary notwithstanding, an oral board wants you to make the best appearance possible. They know you are under pressure – but they also want to see how you respond to it as a guide to what your reaction would be under the pressures of the job you seek. They will be influenced by the degree of poise you display, the personal traits you show and the manner in which you respond.

ABOUT THIS BOOK

This book contains tests divided into Examination Sections. Go through each test, answering every question in the margin. At the end of each test look at the answer key and check your answers. On the ones you got wrong, look at the right answer choice and learn. Do not fill in the answers first. Do not memorize the questions and answers, but understand the answer and principles involved. On your test, the questions will likely be different from the samples. Questions are changed and new ones added. If you understand these past questions you should have success with any changes that arise. Tests may consist of several types of questions. We have additional books on each subject should more study be advisable or necessary for you. Finally, the more you study, the better prepared you will be. This book is intended to be the last thing you study before you walk into the examination room. Prior study of relevant texts is also recommended. NLC publishes some of these in our Fundamental Series. Knowledge and good sense are important factors in passing your exam. Good luck also helps. So now study this Passbook, absorb the material contained within and take that knowledge into the examination. Then do your best to pass that exam.

———

EXAMINATION SECTION

EXAMINATION SECTION
TEST 1

DIRECTIONS: Each question or incomplete statement is followed by several suggested answers or completions. Select the one that BEST answers the question or completes the statement. *PRINT THE LETTER OF THE CORRECT ANSWER IN THE SPACE AT THE RIGHT.*

1. To check for the entrance of toxic wastes into a treatment plant, each of the following may be reliably observed as indicators EXCEPT

   A. changes in color of incoming wastewater
   B. waste recording equipment
   C. odors
   D. bulking of sludge in the clarifier

   1.____

2. An increase in _____ could cause a demand for more oxygen in an aeration tank.

   A. inert or inorganic wastes
   B. pH
   C. toxic substances
   D. microorganisms

   2.____

3. Chlorine may be added for hydrogen sulfide control in the

   A. collection lines   B. aeration tank
   C. plant effluent   D. trickling filter

   3.____

4. The range of typical carrying capacities, in gallons per minute, of intermediate pumping stations is

   A. less than 600   B. 200-700
   C. 100-1,600   D. 700-10,000

   4.____

5. A low sulfanator injector vacuum reading could be caused by

   A. missing gasket
   B. high back pressure
   C. high-volume injector flow
   D. wrong orifice

   5.____

6. Before starting a rotating biological contactor process, each of the following should be checked EXCEPT

   A. lubrication   B. biomass
   C. clearance   D. tightness

   6.____

7. The capacity for water or wastewater to neutralize acids is expressed in terms of

   A. pH   B. oxygen demand
   C. alkalinity   D. acidity

   7.____

8. Which of the following is NOT one of the available methods for determining stormwater flow for the purpose of storm sewer design?

   8.____

A. Rainfall and runoff correlation studies
B. Inlet method
C. Hydrograph method
D. Outlet method

9. What is the term for the accumulation of residue that appears on trickling filters and must be removed periodically?　　　9.____

   A. Sludges   B. Slurries   C. Slugs   D. Sloughings

10. A sludge containing a high number of living organisms is referred to as　　　10.____

   A. raw   B. activated   C. primary   D. toxic

11. Which of the following is NOT a plant location where liquid mixing is commonly practiced?　　　11.____

   A. Ponds
   B. Hydraulic jumps in open channels
   C. Pipelines
   D. Venturi flumes

12. Which of the following industries releases primarily inorganic wastes in its effluent?　　　12.____

   A. Paper   B. Petroleum
   C. Gravel washing   D. Dairy

13. Which of the following collection system variables could upset a plant's activated sludge process?　　　13.____

   A. Discharge by industrial cleaning operations
   B. Chlorination of return sludge flows
   C. Decreases in influent flows
   D. Recycling of digester supernatant

14. The second-stage BOD is also referred to as the _____ stage.　　　14.____

   A. carbonaceous   B. pretreatment
   C. flocculation   D. nitrification

15. When organic matter decomposes to form foul-smelling products associated with the lack of free oxygen, this condition is known as　　　15.____

   A. shock loading   B. septicity
   C. sloughing   D. sidestreaming

16. Which type of bacteria has the HIGHEST optimum temperature for treatment?　　　16.____

   A. Mesophilic   B. Cryophilic
   C. Thermophilic   D. Psychrophilic

17. The COD test　　　17.____

   A. estimates the total oxygen consumed
   B. measures the carbon oxygen demand
   C. provides results more quickly than the BOD test
   D. measures only the nitrification oxygen demand

18. Which of the following is NOT considered a major factor that may cause variations in lab   18.____
     test results?

     A. The nature of the material being examined
     B. Testing equipment
     C. Sampling procedures
     D. The quantity of material being examined

19. The treatment process that MOST effectively removes suspended solids from wastewa-   19.____
     ter is

     A. sedimentation   B. flocculation
     C. skimming   D. comminution

20. Which of the following is a thickening alternative in sludge processing?   20.____

     A. Flotation   B. Incineration
     C. Elutriation   D. Wet oxidation

21. The device that continuously adds the flow of wastewater into a plant is the   21.____

     A. aggregate   B. turbidity meter
     C. titrator   D. totalizer

22. Two types of measurement required in connection with the operation of a treatment plant   22.____
     are

     A. effluent and downstream
     B. temperature and dissolved oxygen
     C. in-plant and receiving water
     D. temperature and receiving water

23. You may NOT dispose of excess activated sludge waste from package plants   23.____

     A. at a nearby treatment plant
     B. by anaerobic digestion
     C. by removal by septic tank pumper
     D. by aeration in a holding tank, then deposit in a sanitary landfill

24. What is the term for the combination of activated sludge with raw wastewater in a treat-   24.____
     ment plant?

     A. Median   B. Liquefaction
     C. Effluent   D. Mixed liquor

25. Landfills produce poisonous _____ gas as a byproduct of decomposition.   25.____

     A. methane   B. nitrogen
     C. chlorofluorocarbons   D. argon

KEY (CORRECT ANSWERS)

1.	B		11.	A
2.	D		12.	C
3.	A		13.	A
4.	D		14.	D
5.	B		15.	B
6.	B		16.	C
7.	C		17.	C
8.	D		18.	D
9.	D		19.	B
10.	B		20.	A

21.	D
22.	C
23.	B
24.	D
25.	A

TEST 2

DIRECTIONS: Each question or incomplete statement is followed by several suggested answers or completions. Select the one that BEST answers the question or completes the statement. *PRINT THE LETTER OF THE CORRECT ANSWER IN THE SPACE AT THE RIGHT.*

1. Which of the following types of pumps is a kinetic pump?   1._____

   A. Rotary   B. Piston plunger
   C. Hydraulic ram   D. Blow case

2. What device is used to keep floated solids out of the effluent in dissolved air flotation thickeners?   2._____

   A. Cloth screens   B. Microscreens
   C. Effluent baffles   D. Water sprays

3. The _____ is NOT one of the primary factors affecting the flow of wastewater and sewage in sewers.   3._____

   A. viscosity of the liquid
   B. cross-sectional area of the system conduit
   C. time of day
   D. pipe surface

4. What is the term for washing a digested sludge in the plant effluent?   4._____

   A. Masking   B. Elutriation
   C. Hydrolysis   D. Slaking

5. _____ is NOT an objective in periodically pumping sludge from the primary clarifier to the digester.   5._____

   A. Prevention of pump clogging
   B. Prevention of digester overload
   C. Allowance for thicker sludge pumping
   D. Maintenance of good clarifier conditions

6. The toxic chemical LEAST likely to be encountered by treatment plant operators is(are)   6._____

   A. mercury   B. acids
   C. fluorocarbons   D. bases

7. Which concentration of total dissolved solids, in milligrams per liter, would be the MINIMUM required in order to be considered *strong* in wastewater?   7._____

   A. 250   B. 500   C. 850   D. 1,200

8. What is the term for the treatment process in which a tank or reactor is filled, the water is treated, and the tank is emptied?   8._____

   A. Flocculation   B. Centration
   C. Batch process   D. Pond process

9. The mixing of a compound with water to produce a true chemical reaction is to   9._____

   A. dissolve   B. slake   C. strip   D. hydrate

10. If the difference in elevation between inflow and outflow sewers is greater than 1.5 feet, which device is needed?   10.____

    A. Side weir   B. Drop inlet
    C. Baffles   D. Inlet casting

11. Intermittent releases or discharges of industrial wastes are known as   11.____

    A. slurries   B. slugs   C. splashes   D. stop logs

12. Results from the settleability test of activated sludge solids may be used to   12.____

    A. calculate BOD
    B. determine probable flow rates at which sludges may clog equipment
    C. calculate sludge age
    D. determine ability of solids to separate from liquid in final clarifier

13. The device used to measure the temperature of an effluent is a   13.____

    A. thermometer   B. Bourdon tube
    C. thermocouple   D. pug mill

14. Which source is typically the HEAVIEST contributor of total solids in a service area's wastewater supply?   14.____

    A. Industrial wastes   B. Domestic wash waters
    C. Storm runoff   D. Human biological wastes

15. The term for liquid removed from a settled sludge is   15.____

    A. hydrolyte   B. supernatant
    C. aliquot   D. slurry

16. A unit of wastewater moving through the treatment system without dispersing or mixing with the rest of the wastewater in the system is called   16.____

    A. centration   B. plug flow
    C. putrefaction   D. slugging

17. What is the term for the groups or clumps of bacteria or particles that have clustered together during the treatment process?   17.____

    A. Coagulants   B. Slurries
    C. Floes   D. Slugs

18. The purpose of PRIMARY sedimentation is to remove   18.____

    A. settleable and floatable material
    B. roots, rags, and large debris
    C. suspended and dissolved solids
    D. sand and gravel

19. _____ would NOT cause an increase in effluent coliform levels at a treatment plant.   19.____

    A. Mixing problems
    B. An increase in effluent BOD
    C. Solids accumulation in the contact chamber
    D. High chlorine residual

20. What is the term used to describe bacteria that can live under either aerobic or anaerobic conditions?   20.____

    A. Cultured   B. Agglomerated
    C. Filamentous   D. Facultative

21. Which devices are NOT used during pretreatment?   21.____

    A. Racks   B. Comminutors
    C. Screens   D. Coagulators

22. Through which stage in an activated sludge treatment plant would wastewater pass FIRST?   22.____

    A. Grit chambers   B. Bar racks
    C. Settling tanks   D. Primary sedimentation

23. The inorganic gas LEAST likely to be found around a treatment plant is   23.____

    A. ammonia   B. methane
    C. hydrogen sulfide   D. mercaptans

24. The soils in an effluent disposal on land program may be tested using each of the following procedures EXCEPT   24.____

    A. BOD   B. conductivity
    C. pH   D. cation exchange capacity

25. Which of the following is a conditioning alternative in sludge processing?   25.____

    A. Centrifugation   B. Drying
    C. Composing   D. Elutriation

KEY (CORRECT ANSWERS)

1.	C	11.	B
2.	C	12.	D
3.	C	13.	C
4.	B	14.	A
5.	A	15.	B
6.	C	16.	B
7.	C	17.	C
8.	C	18.	A
9.	B	19.	D
10.	B	20.	D

21.	D
22.	B
23.	D
24.	A
25.	D

EXAMINATION SECTION
TEST 1

DIRECTIONS: Each question or incomplete statement is followed by several suggested answers or completions. Select the one that BEST answers the question or completes the statement. *PRINT THE LETTER OF THE CORRECT ANSWER IN THE SPACE AT THE RIGHT.*

1. To measure the diameter of a replacement pump shaft, a(n) _____ should be used.   1._____

      A. surveyor's chain   B. micrometer
      C. metallic tape   D. engineer's scale

2. A _____ is used to bypass storm flow in a combined-sewerage system.   2._____

      A. drop inlet   B. side weir
      C. hydraulic jump   D. baffle

3. The PRIMARY element in a control system is the   3._____

      A. transmitter   B. receiver
      C. sensor   D. controller

4. The use of water to break down complex substances into simpler ones is called   4._____

      A. dissolving   B. hydrolysis
      C. coagulation   D. hydrostasis

5. In its progress through a pumping station, wastewater FIRST passes through a   5._____

      A. comminutor   B. chlorine room
      C. wet well   D. barminutor

6. Which of the following is NOT one of the main operational factors for a barminutor?   6._____

      A. Amount of debris in wastewater
      B. Number of units in service
      C. Head loss through unit
      D. Removal of floatables

7. Which of the following precautions must be taken before attempting to repair a surface aerator?   7._____

      A. Shut down aerator
      B. Drain aeration tank
      C. Secure header assembly
      D. Test atmosphere for toxic gases

8. Which of the following source types would MOST likely influence the pH of wastewater?   8._____

      A. Industrial   B. Commercial
      C. Agricultural   D. Domestic

9. Each of the following items should be carefully controlled in an activated sludge plant in order to prevent sludge bulking EXCEPT   9._____

      A. filamentous growth   B. length of aeration time
      C. return sludge rate   D. sludge age

10. Sludge blanket depths may be measured by the use of   10.____

    A. ultrasonic transmitters and receivers
    B. pressure gages
    C. floats connected to cables
    D. bubbler tubes

11. The vertical distance from the normal water surface to the top of the confining wall of a   11.____
pond or tank is called the

    A. freeboard   B. force main
    C. header   D. stop log

12. Suspended solids in the effluent from a trickling filter plant may be caused by   12.____

    A. heavy sloughing from the filters
    B. precipitation of solids in the secondary filter
    C. condensation of effluent on secondary equipment
    D. flotation of solids in the primary clarifier

13. What is MOST often produced during the decomposition of domestic wastes?   13.____

    A. Phenols   B. Oxygen
    C. Hydrogen sulfide   D. Sulfur

14. Air compressor vibration sensing devices are used to measure each of the following   14.____
EXCEPT

    A. flow   B. velocity
    C. acceleration   D. displacement

15. The height or energy of liquids above a certain point is measured in terms of   15.____

    A. discharge rate   B. volume
    C. flow   D. head

16. Factors in the design of sanitary sewers include each of the following EXCEPT   16.____

    A. maximum rate for an entire service area's domestic sewage within a specified time
       period
    B. maximum rates from commercial and industrial areas
    C. infiltration allowance for entire service area
    D. maximum rates from domestic and industrial/commercial sources combined

17. Which of the following could prevent a pump from starting?   17.____

    A. Tripped circuit breakers
    B. Air leaks in suction line
    C. High discharge head
    D. Lack of priming

18. Through which stage would wastewater undergoing chemical-physical treatment pass   18.____
FIRST?

    A. Precipitation   B. Stripping
    C. Flocculation   D. Slaking

19. Which of the following could be considered a normal operating condition for micro-screens?   19.____

  A. High flow   B. High pH level
  C. Low pH flow   D. Toxic wastes

20. The tank in which sludges are placed in order to allow decomposition is known as the   20.____

  A. emulsion   B. dessicator
  C. digester   D. percolator

21. The conversion of large solid sludge particles into fine particles that can be dissolved or suspended in water is called   21.____

  A. hydrolysis   B. liquefaction
  C. comminution   D. recirculation

22. A mixture in which two or more liquid substances are held in suspension is called a(n)   22.____

  A. solution   B. electrolyte
  C. emulsion   D. reagent

23. What is the term for a mass of sludge containing a highly concentrated population of microorganisms?   23.____

  A. Septic   B. Seed
  C. Shock load   D. Slug

24. Which of the following forms of nitrogen is LEAST important to the wastewater treatment process?   24.____

  A. Nitrate   B. Ammonia   C. Elemental   D. Organic

25. What is the term for water leaving a centrifuge after the removal of most solids?   25.____

  A. Cation exchange   B. Centration
  C. Flocculation   D. Turbidity

KEY (CORRECT ANSWERS)

1.	B		11.	A
2.	B		12.	A
3.	C		13.	C
4.	B		14.	A
5.	C		15.	D
6.	D		16.	D
7.	A		17.	A
8.	A		18.	C
9.	D		19.	D
10.	A		20.	C

21. B
22. C
23. B
24. C
25. B

———

TEST 2

1. The MOST effective treatment process for destroying or removing bacteria from waste-water is through

    A. activated sludge process
    B. trickling filter
    C. chlorination
    D. sedimentation

1.____

2. Which of the following tasks is NOT associated with the starting of a comminutor?

    A. Check positioning of inlet and outlet gases
    B. Inspect for frayed cables
    C. Adjust cutter blades
    D. Inspect for lubrication and oil leaks

2.____

3. One of the objectives of digester mixing is

    A. the use of waste gas to run mixers
    B. adequate cooling throughout digester contents
    C. the release of hydrogen sulfide gas
    D. microorganic inoculation of raw sludge

3.____

4. Which type of bacteria would give the STRONGEST indication of the possible presence of pathogenic bacteria in waste-water?

    A. Coliform   B. Filamentous
    C. Heterotrophic   D. Facultative

4.____

5. Cryogenic oxygen plants should be shut down for maintenance every

    A. six months   B. year
    C. two years   D. five years

5.____

6. At the _____ stage in the biological treatment process, aerobic bacteria uses dissolved oxygen to convert carbon compounds to carbon dioxide.

    A. clarifying   B. carbonaceous
    C. nitrification   D. coagulation

6.____

7. _____ is NOT an influential factor in the settleability of solids in a clarifier.

    A. Detention time
    B. Flow velocity
    C. The movement of sludge scrapers
    D. Temperature

7.____

8. Which concentration of total organic carbon, in milligrams per liter, would be considered *moderate* in wastewater?   8.____

    A. 50   B. 100   C. 200   D. 300

9. Which of the following is a volume reduction alternative in sludge processing?   9.____

    A. Centrifugation   B. Chemical conditioning
    C. Flotation   D. Drying

10. The hydraulic loading for a phosphate stripper depends on the   10.____

    A. dissolved oxygen of the activated sludge
    B. pH of wastewater
    C. BOD loading of the unit
    D. ability of the aerobic phosphate stripper to remain aerobic

11. The range of typical carrying capacities, in gallons per minute, of package-plant pumping stations is   11.____

    A. less than 600   B. 200-700
    C. 100-1,600   D. 700-10,000

12. When a sludge becomes too light and refuses to settle properly in a clarifier, this is known as   12.____

    A. centration   B. precipitation
    C. comminution   D. bulking

13. In a wet well, level control systems include each of the following EXCEPT   13.____

    A. bubblers   B. hearts   C. floats   D. electrodes

14. Which of the following is NOT one of the primary sources of odors in a wastewater treatment plant?   14.____

    A. Unwashed grit
    B. The carbon adsorption process
    C. Sludge incinerators
    D. Waste-gas burning

15. A chemical property used in the classification of irrigation waters is   15.____

    A. pH   B. total dissolved solids
    C. BOD   D. aeration

16. Which of the following is NOT a potential use for the dissolved air flotation process?   16.____

    A. Solids recovery   B. Coagulation
    C. Wastewater treatment   D. Water recovery

17. Each of the following is a principal factor determining the use of pumping stations in sewage collection EXCEPT the   17.____

    A. elevation of the area or district to be serviced
    B. location of natural drainage areas in relation to the service area
    C. cost of a pumping station
    D. cost of trunk sewer construction

18. Through which stage would wastewater undergoing chemical-physical treatment pass LAST?   18.____

    A. Carbon adsorption   B. Lime recovery
    C. Flocculation   D. Slaking

19. Which of the following practices is NOT included in the maintenance of equipment in package operation plants?   19.____

    A. Changing oil in the speed reducer
    B. Adjusting aeration equipment
    C. Washing tank walls and channels
    D. Inspecting the air-lift pump

20. What chemical solution is capable of neutralizing acids or bases without greatly altering pH?   20.____
A(n)

    A. blank   B. alkaline   C. buffer   D. digester

21. Which of the following types of pumps is a displacement pump?   21.____

    A. Centrifugal   B. Electromagnetic
    C. Peripheral   D. Diaphragm

22. A sludge whose solid portion can be separated from the liquid is referred to as   22.____

    A. anhydrous   B. soluble
    C. hydrolytic   D. dewaterable

23. Which of the following could indicate that a high organic waste load has reached the activated sludge process?   23.____
A(n)

    A. *increase* in DO residual in the aeration tank
    B. *increase* in turbidity in the effluent from the secondary chamber
    C. *decrease* in nutrients in the effluent from the secondary chamber
    D. *decrease* in aeration

24. The term for the clogging of the filtering medium or a microscreen or a vacuum filter is   24.____

    A. corrosion   B. head loss
    C. coagulation   D. blinding

25. Through which stage in an activated sludge treatment plant would wastewater pass LAST?   25.____

    A. Grit chamber
    B. Chlorine contact chamber
    C. Settling tanks
    D. Trickling filters

KEY (CORRECT ANSWERS)

1.	C		11.	B
2.	B		12.	D
3.	D		13.	B
4.	A		14.	B
5.	B		15.	B
6.	B		16.	B
7.	C		17.	C
8.	C		18.	A
9.	D		19.	A
10.	A		20.	C

21.	D
22.	D
23.	B
24.	D
25.	B

———

EXAMINATION SECTION
TEST 1

DIRECTIONS: Each question or incomplete statement is followed by several suggested answers or completions. Select the one that BEST answers the question or completes the statement. *PRINT THE LETTER OF THE CORRECT ANSWER IN THE SPACE AT THE RIGHT.*

1. The direction of rotation of a d.c. shunt motor can be reversed by reversing   1._____

    A. the line leads
    B. both the armature and field current
    C. the field or armature current
    D. the current in one pole winding

2. The insulation resistance of the stator winding of an induction motor is MOST commonly   2._____
   measured or tested with a(n)

    A. strobe   B. ammeter   C. megger   D. S-meter

3. Assume that three 12-ohm resistances are connected in delta across a 208-volt, 3-phase   3._____
   circuit. The line current, in amperes, will be MOST NEARLY

    A. 30   B. 20.4   C. 17.32   D. 8.66

4. Assume that three 12 ohm resistances are connected in wye across a 208-volt, 3-phase   4._____
   circuit. The power, in watts, dissipated in this resistance load will be MOST NEARLY

    A. 4200   B. 3600   C. 1200   D. 900

5. The one of the following knots which is MOST commonly used to shorten a rope without   5._____
   cutting it is the

    A. clove hitch   B. diamond knot
    C. sheepshank   D. square knot

6. Assume that it is required to pump 40 M.G.D. of water against a 65 ft. head. If the pump   6._____
   efficiency is 65%, the B.H.P. of this pump is MOST NEARLY

    A. 920   B. 700   C. 460   D. 176

7. Assume that a pump had to be shut down temporarily due to trouble which was first   7._____
   reported by an oiler. The one of the following entries in the log concerning this occur-
   rence which is LEAST important is the

    A. time of the shutdown
    B. period of time the pump was out of service
    C. cause of the trouble
    D. time the oiler came on shift

8. At sea level, the theoretical maximum distance, in feet, that water can be lifted by suction   8._____
   only is MOST NEARLY

    A. 12.00   B. 14.70   C. 33.57   D. 72.0

9. While a lubricating oil is in use, for good performance, its neutralization number should   9.____

    A. keep rising
    B. remain about the same
    C. be greater than 0.1
    D. be greater than 2.0

10. Cast iron castings that need repairing are USUALLY repaired by the process known as   10.____

    A. electric arc welding
    B. electro-forming
    C. brazing
    D. resistance welding

11. The term SAE stands for   11.____

    A. Standard Auto Engines
    B. Standard Air Engines
    C. Society of Automotive Engineers
    D. Society of Aviation Engineers

12. The parts of a large sewage pump that would MOST likely need repairs after the least number of hours of operation are the   12.____

    A. pump casings
    B. impellers
    C. wearing rings
    D. outboard bearings

13. Assume that the power in a balanced three-phase load is measured by the two wattmeter method and is read by means of two wattmeters, namely W_1 and W_2. If the power factor of the load is .5 leading,   13.____

    A. W_1 will read positive and W_2 will read negative
    B. W_1 will read negative and W_2 will read positive
    C. both W_1 and W_2 will read negative
    D. W_1 will read positive and W_2 will read zero

14. The current in amperes of a 220-volt 5-H.P., d.c. motor having an efficiency of 90% is MOST NEARLY   14.____

    A. 18.8   B. 17   C. 14.3   D. 20.5

15. A shunt generator having an armature current of 50 amperes, an armature resistance of .05 ohms, and a generated e.m.f. of 222.5 volts will MOST likely have a terminal voltage of _____ volts.   15.____

    A. 172.5   B. 220.0   C. 222.5   D. 225

16. Assume that a 4-pole, 220-volt d.c. motor has a back e.m.f. of 215 volts and 4 armature paths between terminals. If the field flux per pole is suddenly decreased to one-half of its former value, the motor speed, in r.p.m., compared to its original speed will be MOST likely   16.____

    A. decreased to about one-quarter
    B. decreased to about one-half
    C. doubled
    D. increased by one-quarter

17. The frequency of the voltage generated in a synchronous machine having 8 poles and running at 720 r.p.m. is MOST NEARLY   17.____

    A. 120   B. 72   C. 60   D. 48

18. Assume that a synchronous converter has two slip rings and a direct current voltage of 313 volts between the brushes. The effective alternating voltage between slip rings is MOST NEARLY _____ volts.   18.____

    A. 220   B. 278   C. 330   D. 440

19. A newly appointed plant engineer attempted to make an emergency repair on a d.c. motor which had an open armature coil (lap wound) by completely cutting this coil in two and disconnecting it from both commutator bars and then running an insulated jumper large enough to safely carry the current between the two bars. This attempted emergency repair will   19.____

    A. result in an inoperative motor
    B. not significantly affect the normal running of the motor
    C. cause the motor to emit vicious purplish sparks at the commutator while running
    D. cause the motor to overheat excessively while running

20. The purpose of full wave rectifiers is to   20.____

    A. produce a.c. current which contains some d.c.
    B. change d.c. current to a.c.
    C. produce d.c. current having an a.c. ripple of twice the input frequency
    D. produce only a.c. current having twice the input frequency

21. The temporary production of a substitute for a two-phase current so as to obtain a makeshift rotating field in starting a single phase motor is called   21.____

    A. phase splitting   B. pole pitch
    C. phase transformation   D. pole splitting

22. In a fully charged lead acid storage battery, the active material in the positive plates is   22.____

    A. sponge lead   B. lead carbonate
    C. lead acetate   D. lead peroxide

23. A heat exchanger commonly located between the low pressure and high pressure cylinders of an air compressor is used to _____ of the compressor air.   23.____

    A. lower the temperature
    B. increase the relative humidity
    C. decrease the relative humidity
    D. raise the temperature

24. The one of the following instruments which is used for the determination of the velocity of air in ducts is the   24.____

    A. psychrometer   B. pitot tube
    C. *U* gage   D. spherometer

25. A high tension breaker (4160 volts) should be equipped with a mechanical interlock which will prevent the breaker from being raised or advanced into, and lowered or withdrawn from, the operating position unless 25.____

    A. it is open
    B. it is closed
    C. the full load is connected
    D. a light load is connected

26. For the operation of a high tension breaker (4160 volts), the suitable control voltage for BEST performance is usually 26.____

    A. 600 volts a.c.
    C. 208 to 440 volts a.c.
    B. 600 volts d.c.
    D. 70 to 140 volts d.c.

27. The equipment on which you would be MOST likely to find an unloader is a(n) 27.____

    A. centrifugal water pump
    C. vacuum pump
    B. air compressor
    D. steam engine

28. The term Saybolt refers to a measure of 28.____

    A. specific gravity
    C. hardness
    B. boiling point
    D. viscosity

29. Assume that a centrifugal fan running at 750 r.p.m. delivers 20,000 c.f.m. at a static pressure of one inch. If this fan is required to deliver 28,000 c.f.m., at the same static pressure, it should be run at a speed, in r.p.m., of MOST NEARLY 29.____

    A. 1500   B. 1250   C. 1150   D. 1050

30. The horsepower of a fan varies as the _____ of the fan speed. 30.____

    A. cube
    C. square root
    B. square
    D. cube root

31. The gearing for transmitting power between two shafts at right angles to each other consists of two essential parts: 31.____

    A. two worm wheels
    C. a rack and pinion
    B. a worm and bevel gear
    D. two bevel gears

32. If a transmission main drive gear, having 30 teeth, rotates at 400 r.p.m. and drives a counter shaft gear at 300 r.p.m., the total number of teeth on the countershaft drive will be 32.____

    A. 30   B. 40   C. 60   D. 80

33. The one of the following faults of a C.B. main contact which is NOT a cause of overheating of air circuit breakers is 33.____

    A. excessive pressure
    B. insufficient area in contact
    C. oxidized contacts
    D. dirty contacts

34. The MAIN reason that larger size electrical cables (such as #0000) are always stranded rather than solid is that they

    A. are more flexible
    B. are stronger
    C. have a higher conductivity
    D. have a higher specific resistance

34.____

Questions 35-37.

DIRECTIONS: Questions 35 through 37, inclusive, are to be answered in accordance with the diagram of the auto transformer and data below.

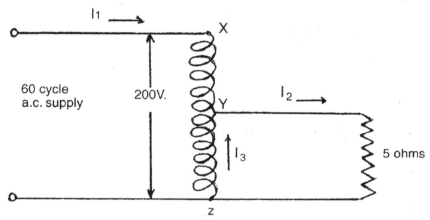

Data: An auto transformer whose primary is XZ is connected across a 200-volt a.c. supply as shown in the above diagram. The load of 5 ohms is connected across Y and Z. (Assume that point Y is the mid-point of the winding.)

35. The current I_1, in amperes, is APPROXIMATELY equal to

    A. 5   B. 10   C. 15   D. 20

35.____

36. The current I_2, in amperes, is APPROXIMATELY equal to

    A. 5   B. 10   C. 15   D. 20

36.____

37. The current I_3, in amperes, is APPROXIMATELY equal to

    A. 5   B. 10   C. 15   D. 20

37.____

38. Assume that you see one of your oilers tumble down a long flight of concrete steps and fall heavily on the lower landing. You rush to him and find that he is unconscious but breathing. Of the following, the BEST course of action for you to take is

    A. have two of your men carry him to the office and summon a doctor
    B. do not move him but cover him with a blanket and call a doctor
    C. prop him upright and let him inhale spirits of ammonia and call a doctor
    D. prepare a bed of blankets and have two of your men lift him on it, then summon a doctor

38.____

39. It is sometimes desirable to have a control that will cause a d.c. motor to come to a standstill quickly instead of coasting to a standstill after the stop button is pressed. This result is MOST commonly obtained by means of an action called

    A. counter e.m.f. method
    B. armature reaction
    C. diverting
    D. dynamic braking

39._____

40. In an electric circuit, a high-spot-temperature is MOST commonly due to

    A. an open circuit
    B. a defective connection
    C. intermittent use of circuit
    D. excessive distribution voltage

40._____

KEY (CORRECT ANSWERS)

1.	C	11.	C	21.	A	31.	D
2.	C	12.	C	22.	D	32.	B
3.	A	13.	D	23.	A	33.	A
4.	B	14.	A	24.	B	34.	A
5.	C	15.	B	25.	A	35.	B
6.	B	16.	C	26.	D	36.	D
7.	D	17.	D	27.	B	37.	B
8.	C	18.	A	28.	D	38.	B
9.	B	19.	B	29.	D	39.	D
10.	C	20.	C	30.	A	40.	B

TEST 2

DIRECTIONS: Each question or incomplete statement is followed by several suggested answers or completions. Select the one that BEST answers the question or completes the statement. *PRINT THE LETTER OF THE CORRECT ANSWER IN THE SPACE AT THE RIGHT.*

1. The MAIN reason for periodic inspections and testing of equipment in an electrically powered plant is to   1.____

    A. keep the men busy at all times
    B. familiarize the men with the equipment
    C. train the men to be ready in an emergency
    D. discover minor faults before they have a chance to become significantly serious

2. Assume that an employee calls up to give advance notice of his intentions to be absent the following day. The MOST important information that he should give is   2.____

    A. the exact time of calling
    B. the balance of his sick leave time
    C. the reason for his absence
    D. name of attending doctor

3. The MAIN reason why a plant mechanic who is assigned to service equipment must be able to make proper adjustments and repairs quickly is that   3.____

    A. equipment always deteriorates rapidly unless readjusted immediately
    B. idle equipment will result in poor plant efficiency and work delays
    C. the ability to work rapidly is the result of extensive training and experience
    D. he will have more time for his other duties

4. A 1300-volt, three-phase system with a grounded neutral has a phase to ground voltage of APPROXIMATELY   4.____

    A. 440   B. 600   C. 690   D. 750

5. A 220-volt, 40-H.P. induction motor is given an insulation resistance test. The normal value of the insulating resistance, in megohms, for this motor is MOST NEARLY   5.____

    A. 0.2   B. 0.4   C. 0.05   D. 0.95

6. To increase the range of an a.c. ammeter, the one of the following which is MOST commonly used is a(n)   6.____

    A. current transformer   B. inductance
    C. condenser   D. straight copper bar

7. When batteries are being charged, they should not be exposed to open flames and sparks because of the flammability of   7.____

    A. hydrogen   B. oxygen
    C. sulphurous gas   D. fuming sulphuric acid

8. Assume that you and your supervisor are on an inspectional tour of the outdoor equip-   8.____
ment of the plant and that a co-worker suddenly falls unconscious on the pavement. If on
close observation you find that the victim is not breathing, the FIRST of the following
things to do is

    A. move the victim indoors
    B. notify his family
    C. administer first aid to restore breathing
    D. nothing, but summon a doctor

9. Assume that one of your men, who has always been efficient, industrious, and conscien-   9.____
tious, suddenly becomes lax in his work, makes numerous mistakes, and shuns
responsibilities. The cause of such a change

    A. is usually that the man is responding to a minor change in the job situation
    B. is usually apparent to the stationary engineer in charge and fellow workers
    C. may be quickly found by a close study of reports and personnel records
    D. may have no direct relationship to any change in the job situation

Questions 10-12.

DIRECTIONS: Questions 10 through 12, inclusive, are to be answered in accordance with the
diagram of a 3-phase transformer and data given below.

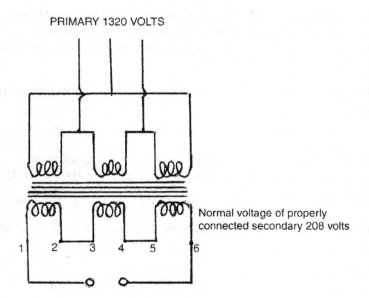

PRIMARY 1320 VOLTS

Normal voltage of properly
connected secondary 208 volts

1 2 3 4 5 6

<u>Data:</u> The above transformer is to be connected delta-delta, with primary connections
completed as shown. Assume that the connections of the secondary of the transformer
bank are not completed and it is found that coil (1-2) is reversed. Under this condition:

10. The voltage between points 6 and 3 will be MOST NEARLY   10.____

    A. 208   B. 360   C. 416   D. 520

11. The voltage between points 1 and 6 will be MOST NEARLY   11.____

    A. 208   B. 360   C. 416   D. 520

12. The voltage between points 1 and 4 will be MOST NEARLY   12.____

    A. 208   B. 360   C. 416   D. 520

13. The one of the following types of valves which is GENERALLY used where extremely   13.____
    close regulation of flow is needed is the _____ valve.

    A. gate   B. glove   C. needle   D. blow-off

14. Lubricating oils of mineral origin are refined from _____ products.   14.____

    A. lard-beef   B. cotton seed
    C. crude petroleum   D. lime soap

Questions 15-17.

DIRECTIONS: Questions 15 through 17, inclusive, are to be answered in accordance with the
               diagram below.

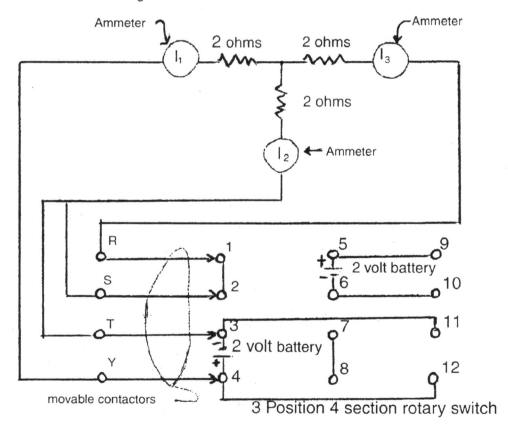

15. When switch movable contactors R, S, T, and V are in position 1, 2, 3, and 4, as shown,   15.____
    the current I_1, in amperes, is MOST NEARLY

    A. 2   B. 2/3   C. 1/3   D. 1/6

16. When switch movable contactors R, S, T, and V are in position 5, 6, 7, and 8, the current I_2, in amperes, is MOST NEARLY   16.____

      A. 2   B. 2/3   C. 1/3   D. 1/6

17. When switch movable contactors R, S, T, and V are in position 9, 10, 11, and 12, the current, in amperes, registered by ammeter I_3 is MOST NEARLY   17.____

      A. 3   B. 2   C. 2/3   D. 1/3

18. Light-bodied lubricating oils are MOST commonly used for   18.____

      A. light loads at high speeds
      B. heavy bearing pressure
      C. heavy loads at slow speeds
      D. chain drives and gears

19. The one of the following lubricants which is LEAST likely to be attacked by acids is   19.____

      A. cottonseed oil   B. castor oil
      C. rape seed oil   D. graphite

20. In general, non-rising stem gate valves are BEST adaptable for   20.____

      A. use where frequent adjustments are necessary
      B. installations carrying viscous liquids
      C. throttling or close control
      D. places where space is a factor

21. The presence of moisture in insulating oil is undesirable. The percentage of moisture which will reduce the dielectric strength of insulating oil to approximately one-half of its dielectric strength when dry is MOST NEARLY _____ of moisture.   21.____

      A. 0.5%   B. 0.05%   C. 0.005%   D. 0.0005%

22. It has been brought to your attention that one of the men under your supervision is complaining to fellow co-workers that another man has received an easy assignment through his *connections*. In this situation, it is BEST to   22.____

      A. privately inform the man who is complaining of the truth regarding the assignment
      B. in the presence of others, demand absolute proof from the man who is complaining
      C. ignore the matter since it is not your job to interfere in disagreements between the men
      D. tell the complaining man to apply for a desirable assignment also

23. In the standard method of testing electrical insulating oils, the test cup used to determine the dielectric strength contains two electrodes, each _____ inch in diameter with a gap of _____ inch between them.   23.____

      A. 0.1; 1   B. 0.5; 0.3   C. 0.75; 0.3   D. 1.00; 0.1

24. The PROPER fire extinguishing agent to use to extinguish fires in electrical equipment is   24.____

      A. water   B. foam
      C. soda-acid   D. carbon dioxide

25. Circuit conductors operating at 600 volts or less may be worked upon live, without open-   25.____
ing the circuit, if certain precautionary measures are taken. The one of the following that
BEST represents one of these precautionary measures for this work is

   A. bare or exposed places on one conductor must be taped after another conductor is
   first exposed
   B. adjacent live or grounded conductor shall be covered with a conducting material
   C. bare or exposed places on one conductor must be taped before another conductor
   is exposed
   D. adjacent live or grounded conductors shall be securely bonded to ground

26. In order to properly distribute the load (in proportion to their rated capacities) between   26.____
two alternators which are operating in parallel, it is necessary to

   A. overexcite the smaller alternator and underexcite the larger one
   B. adjust the governor on the prime mover
   C. underexcite the larger alternator but use normal excitation on the smaller one
   D. underexcite the smaller alternator and overexcite the larger one

27. If a large amount of flame is visible from a small pile of burning material, it is likely that   27.____
the material MUST contain a substance that

   A. contains a large amount of inorganic material
   B. produces during the burning process a large amount of pure carbon
   C. produces during the burning process a large amount of combustible gases or
   vapors
   D. is composed almost entirely of pure carbon

28. If the velocity of water flow in a pipe is doubled, assuming other factors are constant, the   28.____
loss of head due to friction will be

   A. decreased 1/2 times   B. decreased 1/4 times
   C. increased 4 times   D. the same

29. Reprimanding a subordinate for inefficiency in the presence of fellow co-workers is apt to   29.____

   A. cause the subordinate to resign
   B. arouse the subordinate's resentment
   C. improve the performance of all present
   D. cause the subordinate to improve

30. Assume that certain work assignments are not liked by any of your subordinates.   30.____
Because this work has to be done, you, as the operator in charge, should try as much as
possible to

   A. assign this work as punishment details
   B. rotate the work assignments among subordinates
   C. assign this work to the best-natured man
   D. assign this work to the junior men

31. A senior engineer, in discussing new departmental regulations with his subordinates,   31.____
commented, *We should be conscious of the fact that our interests are mutual, and that
by all of us in unison putting our shoulder to the wheel and working together, we can
achieve our common objective.* This approach is

A. *good,* because this attitude will promote cooperation
B. *poor,* because this approach will invite excessive criticism
C. *good,* because it will promote good fellowship
D. *poor,* because this will invite too much familiarity

32. In the inspection of relays, the type of trouble generally encountered often depends on the type of relay. The one of the following which is NOT a trouble encountered with an induction-type relay is   32._____

    A. friction between disc and magnet
    B. dust on disc
    C. foreign matter in the gear train
    D. punctured bellows

33. With reference to diesel engines, the one of the following which is NOT a method of scavenging the cylinder is _____ scavenging.   33._____

    A. crankcase   B. integral
    C. under-piston   D. vane

34. Direct current motors for BEST performance should have their brushes set on the commutator   34._____

    A. at the neutral point (under load)
    B. at the point of maximum armature reaction
    C. radially at an angle of 90 (leading)
    D. radially at an angle of 80 (leading)

35. The PROPER order of events that take place in a 4-stroke cycle diesel engine is _____, and exhaust.   35._____

    A. air intake, power expansion, compression
    B. air intake, compression, power expansion
    C. power expansion, air intake, compression
    D. compression, air intake, power expansion

36. The compression ratio of a diesel engine that has no starting ignition device is GENERALLY in the range of   36._____

    A. 11 to 20   B. 8 to 10   C. 6 to 8   D. 4 to 6

37. The base in a lubricating grease denotes the   37._____

    A. type of soap that is used in its manufacture
    B. consistency and the texture of the grease
    C. dropping or melting point of the grease
    D. carbon-residue content of the grease

38. Of the following sets of pipes, the one having a total combined area exactly equal to the area of a 12" diameter pipe is _____ pipes.   38._____

    A. two 6"   B. two 8"
    C. one 8" pipe and two 6"   D. four 6"

39. Assume that a single phase load takes EI x .8 watts, where E is the line voltage, I the line current, and .8 the power factor. The rating in volt-amperes of the synchronous condenser needed to raise the power factor to unity is MOST NEARLY EI x   39.____

    A. .6   B. .8   C. .9   D. 1

40. If rubber gloves commonly used on high tension work are found on test to have pinholes, they   40.____

    A. may be used on low voltage
    B. should be discarded
    C. should be patched with rubber tape
    D. may be used only in dry places

KEY (CORRECT ANSWERS)

1. D	11. C	21. C	31. A
2. C	12. B	22. A	32. D
3. B	13. C	23. D	33. D
4. D	14. C	24. D	34. A
5. A	15. B	25. C	35. B
6. A	16. C	26. B	36. A
7. A	17. D	27. C	37. A
8. C	18. A	28. C	38. D
9. D	19. D	29. B	39. A
10. A	20. D	30. B	40. B

EXAMINATION SECTION
TEST 1

DIRECTIONS: Each question or incomplete statement is followed by several suggested answers or completions. Select the one that BEST answers the question or completes the statement. *PRINT THE LETTER OF THE CORRECT ANSWER IN THE SPACE AT THE RIGHT.*

1. Assume that one of the men under your supervision asks you a technical question to which you do not know the answer.
   Of the following, it is BEST that you

   A. tell him that you do not know the answer but that you will get the information for him
   B. tell him to find out for himself
   C. bluff him by giving him an answer
   D. pretend that you are needed elsewhere urgently and avoid giving an answer

   1._____

2. In ordering standard cartridge fuses, it is necessary to specify only the

   A. voltage of the circuit
   B. current capacity of the circuit and the power to be dissipated
   C. power to be dissipated
   D. current capacity and the voltage of the circuit

   2._____

3. A synchronous motor having 12 poles and operating on 60-cycle alternating current would have a speed, in r.p.m., of MOST NEARLY

   A. 300   B. 360   C. 600   D. 720

   3._____

4. In a fully charged lead acid storage battery, the active material of the plates is

   A. lead peroxide on the positive and sponge lead on the negative plates
   B. lead peroxide on the positive and the negative plates
   C. sponge lead on the positive and the negative plates
   D. lead peroxide on the negative and sponge lead on the positive plates

   4._____

5. Assume that a three-phase wound rotor induction motor is running at full speed and no load when the connection between the windings and one of the collector rings suddenly breaks.
   Under this condition, the motor will

   A. immediately stop
   B. continue to run at full speed but will slow down when the load is added
   C. continue to run at full speed but will overheat
   D. run at half speed

   5._____

6. Of the following, the PRIMARY function of a pyrometer is to measure

   A. revolutions per minute   B. synchronization
   C. gallons per minute   D. temperature

   6._____

7. In general, the temperature of a gas or vapor compressed in a limited space will

   A. increase
   B. decrease

   7._____

C. decrease and then gradually increase
D. remain the same

8. Assume that the stem of a large valve has multiple threads. Of the following, the BEST reason for using multiple threads in this instance is to   8._____

A. decrease the length of travel of the stem
B. permit the valve to be opened or closed faster
C. reduce the friction due to corrosion
D. prevent backlash

9. Of the following, the valve generally used where accurate throttling is required such as for instrument, gage, or meter line service is the _____ valve.   9._____

A. butterfly   B. globe
C. needle   D. O.S. and Y.

10. Of the following, the one which is NOT part of a safe, well-planned, lockout procedure is   10._____

A. no two locks should be the same
B. furnish all plant personnel with identical padlocks and keys
C. each key should fit only one lock
D. duplicate sets of keys not to be readily accessible to the worker in case a key is lost

11. Of the following, the one which shows the BEST supervisory conduct is   11._____

A. assume credit for a subordinate's ideas
B. admit your mistakes
C. never be friendly with your subordinates
D. gain respect by losing your temper occasionally

12. Of the following, the BEST practical way to keep morale high among the men/women he supervises is to   12._____

A. individually assist the men/women on all of their jobs
B. praise the men/women when they do a good job
C. reward good work with special privileges
D. give good workers the best jobs

13. Of the following, the BEST procedure to use when it becomes necessary to reprimand a worker is to   13._____

A. reprimand him in private rather than in public, even if you must wait a day
B. avoid speaking directly about the problem so as not to insult the worker
C. be fair and give the identical reprimand to all workers rather than change it to suit the individual involved
D. always reprimand the worker immediately to prevent others from making the same mistake

14. Assume that you have told one of your men how to do a certain job. While you are absent, your supervisor checks on the job and gives this man different orders. Of the following, it would be BEST for you to   14._____

A. talk the matter over with your boss privately
B. tell the man that he should have told the supervisor to see you first

C. always check with your supervisor in the future before issuing orders
D. tell your men to always follow your orders without change

15. You feel that the morale of your crew would improve if they were permitted to demon-   15._____
strate their skills and prove their ability.
Of the following, the condition under which it is LEAST likely that you will achieve this
goal is if they

A. all have similar skills
B. are frequently trained to use new equipment and learn new techniques
C. are closely supervised
D. are required to do relatively complex tasks using their own initiative

16. Of the following, the MOST important step in the process of training a worker to perform   16._____
a new task is

A. explain what to do and how to do it
B. show what to do and how to do it
C. have the workers practice the task under supervision
D. make sure the worker understands why he is doing it

17. Of the following, the one which is NOT a distinguishing feature of a *preventive* mainte-   17._____
nance program is

A. periodic inspection to uncover potential trouble
B. diligent adjustment and repair of minor troubles
C. obtain and keep records of normal operating temperatures, pressures, etc., and
investigate any changes
D. make only those repairs necessary to get equipment back into service

18. The direction of rotation of a DC shunt motor can be reversed by reversing   18._____

A. both the field and the armature connections
B. either the field or the armature connections
C. the line connections
D. the residual field

19. The insulation on high voltage cables must be capable of resisting the gas sometimes   19._____
produced by electrical action in the vicinity of high voltage.
This gas is called

A. freon   B. oxygen   C. neon   D. ozone

20. A 5-volt voltmeter has a resistance of 500 ohms.   20._____
Of the following resistances, the one which should be placed in series with this instrument in order to measure voltages up to 150 volts is _____ ohms.

A. 75,000   B. 14,500   C. 2,500   D. 750

21. Assume that a certain 120-volt single-phase AC circuit draws a current of 12 amperes   21._____
and a wattmeter in the circuit reads 1150 watts.
The power factor, in percent, of this circuit is MOST NEARLY

A. 75   B. 80   C. 85   D. 95

4 (#1)

22. If the voltage between lines in a 3-phase, 4-wire system is 4160 volts, the voltage to neutral is MOST NEARLY   22.____

    A. 2400   B. 2080   C. 1380   D. 1200

23. Assume that the contacts of an air circuit breaker flash from one to the other.   23.____
    Of the following troubles, the one which is MOST likely to cause these symptoms is

    A. overload relays set low
    B. overheating
    C. closing coil circuit open
    D. barriers broken

24. The term *trip-free* applies to a circuit breaker that   24.____

    A. cannot be tripped when the operating lever is held in the closed position
    B. can be tripped only by the operator
    C. can be tripped by the overload mechanism even though the operating lever is held in the closed position
    D. is tripped from a shunt-circuit relay

25. The insulation resistance of a certain rubber-insulated single conductor cable 2200 feet   25.____
    long is 360 megohms.
    If a 1100-foot section of this cable is cut off, it will have an insulation resistance, in megohms, of MOST NEARLY

    A. 1400   B. 720   C. 180   D. 90

26. When the level of the electrolyte in a lead-acid storage battery has fallen below the top of   26.____
    the plates, the MOST preferred of the following actions is to raise the electrolyte level
    _____ charging by adding _____.

    A. before; water   B. after; water
    C. before; sulfuric acid   D. after; sulfuric acid

27. The gases usually generated by electrolytic action while charging a lead-acid storage   27.____
    battery are

    A. sulfur dioxide and lead sulphate
    B. hydrogen and chlorine
    C. hydrogen and oxygen
    D. chlorine and oxygen

28. On a DC generator, the polarity of an interpole is the same as that of the _____ in the   28.____
    direction of rotation.

    A. interpole preceding it,   B. main pole it follows,
    C. main pole it precedes,   D. interpole following it,

29. The distance between the center lines of adjacent north and south poles, measured   29.____
    along the circumference at the armature surface of an alternator, is called the

    A. stator pitch   B. pole circumference
    C. pole pitch   D. pitch factor

34

30. Compensator starters for polyphase squirrel cage motors are basically   30.____

    A. autotransformers
    B. resistance banks
    C. delta-wye switches
    D. QMQB across-the-line switches

31. In general, the power factor of a polyphase squirrel cage induction motor will   31.____

    A. increase if the load increases
    B. decrease if the load increases
    C. increase if the load decreases
    D. remain the same regardless of the load

32. A certain pumping station uses five large centrifugal pumps. Three are driven by wound   32.____
    rotor induction motors, and two are driven by synchronous motors.
    The MAIN reason for this combination is that

    A. wound rotor induction motors can be used to improve the power factor
    B. synchronous motors can be used to provide flexibility due to speed variation
    C. synchronous motors can be used to improve the power factor
    D. wound rotor induction motors are used because their speed is absolutely constant

33. Assume that the input of a certain motor is 32,000 watts and its losses are 4,000 watts.   33.____
    The efficiency, in percent, of this motor is MOST NEARLY

    A. 88.8   B. 87.5   C. 81.3   D. 77.7

34. After repairs to the electrical supply, a three-phase, 3-wire, AC wound rotor induction   34.____
    motor is found to rotate in the wrong direction.
    In order to reverse the direction of rotation, it is necessary to

    A. reverse the field connections
    B. reverse any two supply lines connected to the stator
    C. reverse two leads connected to the rotor
    D. change the phase rotation of the rotor leads

35. Assume that several three-phase induction motors which are supplied through the same   35.____
    oil circuit breaker all hum but will not start,
    Of the following troubles, the one that is MOST likely to be responsible for such a situation is

    A. the fuse of one motor is blown
    B. one set of breaker contacts is so badly burned that they do not complete the connection
    C. all contacts of the circuit breaker are welded shut
    D. tripping mechanism of breaker is jammed so that trip coil pistons do not release toggle

36. In order to determine the no-load speed of a wound rotor induction motor, the load MUST   36.____
    be disconnected and the motor run with

    A. resistance equal to the rotor resistance in series with the stator leads
    B. resistance equal to the stator resistance in the rotor

C. the rotor resistance all in
D. the rotor resistance short-circuited

37. Assume that a certain AC motor is started by means of a compensator. At times, although the motor is not overloaded, the fuse blows when the operator throws the compensator from the starting to the running position. Of the following, the action MOST likely to cause this trouble is that the operator throws the starting switch of the compensator to the running position

37.____

A. with the main switch closed
B. too slowly
C. too quickly
D. with the main switch open

38. Of the following, the BEST use for a one-to-one transformer is to

38.____

A. electrically isolate the load from the source of supply
B. connect voltmeters to high voltage circuits
C. change from three-phase to two-phase
D. connect voltmeters to low voltage circuits

39. Assume that an auto transformer draws 25 amperes from a 400-volt line in order to supply 100 amperes at 100 volts to a load.
The current flowing in that portion of the auto transformer winding across which the load is connected is _____ amperes.

39.____

A. 125   B. 75   C. 100   D. 20

40. Of the following, the MOST important precaution that should be observed in using a current instrument transformer is to

40.____

A. open the primary circuit after opening the secondary
B. open the secondary circuit with the primary energized
C. short circuit the primary after opening the secondary circuit
D. short circuit the secondary prior to opening the secondary circuit

KEY (CORRECT ANSWERS)

1.	A	11.	B	21.	B	31.	A
2.	D	12.	B	22.	A	32.	C
3.	C	13.	A	23.	D	33.	B
4.	A	14.	A	24.	C	34.	B
5.	D	15.	C	25.	B	35.	B
6.	D	16.	C	26.	A	36.	D
7.	A	17.	D	27.	C	37.	C
8.	B	18.	B	28.	B	38.	A
9.	C	19.	D	29.	C	39.	B
10.	B	20.	B	30.	A	40.	D

TEST 2

DIRECTIONS: Each question or incomplete statement is followed by several suggested answers or completions. Select the one that BEST answers the question or completes the statement. *PRINT THE LETTER OF THE CORRECT ANSWER IN THE SPACE AT THE RIGHT.*

1. Assume that three single-phase transformers each have a primary rated at 2400 volts and a secondary rated at 480 volts.
   In order to obtain a 480 volt 3-wire 3-phase service from a 4160 volt supply line, these transformers should be connected in   1._____

   A. delta-wye   B. wye-wye
   C. delta-delta   D. wye-delta

2. Assume that the full rating of a certain transformer is 190 kw at *95%* power factor.
   The kva rating of this transformer is MOST NEARLY   2._____

   A. 95   B. 200   C. 180   D. 220

3. Assume that a load totaling 500 kw is to be supplied. Two 500 kw generators and one 250 kw generator are available.
   Of the following combinations, the MOST efficient operation would be achieved by operating   3._____

   A. one 500 kw machine at full load
   B. both 500 kw machines at half load
   C. both 500 dw machines at 200 kw load and the 250 kw machine at 100 kw load
   D. one 500 kw machine at half load and the 250 kw machine at full load

4. Assume that the power in a balanced three-wire, three-phase load is measured by the two wattmeter method and is read by means of two wattmeters, W_1 and W2.
   If W_1/W_2 is positive, decreases to zero and then becomes negative, the power factor has changed from   4._____

   A. lagging to leading
   B. leading to lagging
   C. a value below .5 to a value above .5
   D. a value above .5 to a value below .5

5. Assume that it is required to measure the power in an unbalanced varying three-phase, four-wire, 120/208 volt circuit directly.
   Of the following sets of instruments, the one indicating the minimum number required for this is   5._____

   A. an ammeter and a voltmeter
   B. two wattmeters
   C. three wattmeters
   D. four wattmeters

6. Assume that a certain standard cartridge fuse is loose in its clips. This will result in the

   6._____

  A. fuse blowing as soon as the full power is turned on
  B. clips becoming hot
  C. fuse blowing out when half of the normal voltage is used
  D. creation of a ground on the circuit

7. Assume that only one of the following instruments is available to measure a certain insulation resistance. Of these, the BEST choice is _____ resistance.

   7._____

  A. ammeter of high   B. voltmeter of low
  C. ammeter of low   D. voltmeter of high

8. If the speed of the prime mover driving the alternator supplying a synchronous motor becomes unstable, the motor will

   8._____

  A. job   B. plug
  C. overcompound   D. hunt

9. The type of meter used to indicate the phase relation between the voltage and the current of an AC circuit is called a

   9._____

  A. phase meter   B. phase difference meter
  C. power factor meter   D. a synchroscope

10. Assume that a circuit breaker equipped with a bellows-type plunger time delay relay opens instantaneously an overload although set for a certain time delay during the last inspection.
The MOST likely cause is

   10._____

  A. contacts pitted
  B. air vent completely closed
  C. air vent wide open
  D. disk rubbing

11. Assume that there is unequal heating in a bank of transformers connected wye primary and delta secondary.
Of the following troubles, the one which can cause these symptoms is

   11._____

  A. overload
  B. ground on one of the primary phases
  C. not sufficient oil in tank
  D. oil saponified on outside of cooling coils

12. Assume that a 3-phase 3-wire 4160 volt system has a balanced three-phase load connected to it and that the kva of the load is to be measured by means of an ammeter and voltmeter connected through instrument transformers. The CT is rated 200/5 amperes and the PT is rated 4160/120. If the voltmeter reads 100 volts and the ammeter reads 4.8 amperes, the load, in kva, is MOST NEARLY

   12._____

  A. 1152   B. 33.5   C. 670   D. 8.4

13. Of the following, the one which is an accurate and convenient method of measuring liquid velocity is a   13.____

    A. pitotmeter   B. dynamometer
    C. liquidometer   D. piezometer

14. In a venturi meter, the liquid flows from a large section into a narrow throat. In such a meter, the flow of liquid from the large section to the throat is _____ its static pressure _____ .   14.____

    A. accelerated and; is increased
    B. accelerated and; is reduced
    C. decreased and; is increased
    D. accelerated but; remains the same

15. Of the following statements concerning the oiling of ring-oiled bearings on electric motors, the one which describes the BEST procedure is that ring-oiled bearings should be filled through the   15.____

    A. filler gauge on the side of the bearing housing when the machine is shut down
    B. top when the machine is shut down
    C. top when the machine is running
    D. filler gauge when the machine is running

16. Assume that a vacuum gauge reads 24" of mercury. This is equivalent to an absolute pressure of MOST NEARLY _____ p.s.i.   16.____

    A. 11.8   B. 6.0   C. 8.7   D. 2.9

17. Of the following, the one which BEST describes the function of a prony brake is   17.____

    A. prevent series motors from *running away*
    B. bring prime movers to a very rapid stop
    C. measure the power output of motors
    D. regenerative braking of DC motors

18. Assume that a spur gear having 60 teeth revolves at 720 r.p.m. that drives another spur gear having 80 teeth. The speed, in r.p.m., at which the gear having 80 teeth revolves will be   18.____

    A. 270   B. 540   C. 480   D. 960

19. In an ordering description for a 6" gate valve, it is specified that the valve shall be: I.B.B.M.; O.S.&Y.; and F.E.
Of the following, the one that MOST NEARLY defines these abbreviations is iron   19.____

    A. and brass body mounted, open stem and yoke, flanged end
    B. body brass mounted, open stem and yoke, fluted end
    C. body brass mounted, open stem and yoke, flanged end
    D. body brass mounted, open seat and yoke, flanged end

20. The surge caused by sudden opening or closing of valves in a closed liquid piping system is USUALLY called   20.____

    A. jetting   B. precipitation
    C. water hammer   D. tailing

21. Of the following, the MOST likely location for an *after-cooler* on a super-charged dual fuel diesel engine is

    A. between the turbocharger and the intake manifold
    B. in the fuel injection system
    C. between the lubricating oil filter and the sump tank
    D. in the day tank

21._____

22. Dual-fuel diesel engines USUALLY require

    A. afterburners
    B. carburetors
    C. spark plugs to initiate ignition
    D. pilot injection of liquid fuel to initiate ignition

22._____

23. Assume that an engine has a no-load speed of 370 r.p.m. and a full load speed of 360 r.p.m.
The speed regulation of this engine is MOST NEARLY

    A. .98%   B. 2.2%   C. 1.1%   D. 2.75%

23._____

24. Assume that a given centrifugal pump requires 100 h.p. when operating at 1000 r.p.m. A required increase in the capacity and the head makes it necessary to operate at 1100 r.p.m.
Under these conditions, the required power is MOST NEARLY _____ HP.

    A. 101   B. 123   C. 110   D. 133

24._____

25. Assume that 60,000 gpm of water at 60F are to be raised through a lift of 33 feet.
If the efficiency of the pump is 50% and a gallon of water weighs 8.3 pounds, then the horsepower required to drive the pump is MOST NEARLY

    A. 600   B. 1000   C. 800   D. 1200

25._____

26. Assume that a certain pumping station has three pumps A, B, and C. A can pump 1000 gallons in 6 minutes, B can pump 1000 gallons in 3 minutes, and C can pump 1000 gallons in 2 minutes.
The time required for all three pumps, working at the same time, to pump 1000 gallons is MOST NEARLY _____ minute(s).

    A. 2   B. 1   C. 1 1/2   D. 1/2

26._____

27. Assume that a centrifugal pump that is used to pump water has a water seal ring in its stuffing box.
Of the following, the MAIN purpose of the water seal ring in such a case is to prevent

    A. water from leaking out of the pump into the stuffing box
    B. water from getting into the packing
    C. air from entering the pump through the packing box
    D. water from leaking out of the stuffing box

27._____

28. For a given centrifugal pump, the quantity of water delivered will vary _____ the speed.

    A. directly as
    B. inversely as

28._____

C. directly as the square of
D. inversely as the square of

29. Assume that two identical centrifugal pumps are operated in series.   29._____
Under these conditions, the _____ at which they operate together at a given _____ .

    A. capacity; head is a quarter of that for a single pump
    B. head; capacity is double that for a single pump
    C. efficiency; capacity is half that for a single pump
    D. capacity; head is double that for a given pump

30. For a given centrifugal pump, the head will vary   30._____

    A. directly as the square root of the speed
    B. directly as the speed
    C. inversely as the speed
    D. directly as the square of the speed

31. Of the following, the MAIN purpose of the volute casing on a centrifugal pump is to   31._____

    A. convert its velocity head into pressure
    B. provide a chamber for priming the pump
    C. aid in venting the pump
    D. convert its pressure head to velocity

32. Of the following types of pumps, the one NOT generally used as a diesel fuel transfer   32._____
pump is the _____ type.

    A. gear   B. screw
    C. lobe   D. reciprocating

33. Of the following oils, the one which is the HEAVIEST is S.A.E.   33._____

    A. 10   B. 30   C. 20   D. 40

34. Of the following, a well-planned safety program should NOT be expected to   34._____

    A. help develop safe work habits and attitudes
    B. focus attention on specific accident causes
    C. compensate for unsafe conditions and procedures
    D. improve employee and management relations

35. Of the following, the one which describes the safest method for using an adjustable   35._____
wrench is with the open jaw facing _____ on the handle.

    A. the user, pull
    B. the user, push
    C. away from the user, pull
    D. away from the user, push

36. Of the following basic techniques for preventing accidental injury, the one which is MOST   36._____
effective is

    A. make the workers aware of the hazard and train them to avoid it
    B. control the hazard by guarding it

C. eliminate the hazard from the plant
D. encourage the use of protective devices to shield the men against the hazard

37. Portable electric power tools permanently marked with the words *double insulated* and which have been so listed by the Underwriters' Laboratories, Inc. can be safely used   37._____

    A. without third wire grounding
    B. only with polarized receptacles
    C. to work on *live* equipment
    D. in areas containing high concentrations of volatilized flammable solvents

38. When using a two-section extension ladder with an extended length of 60 feet, the one of the following which is NOT a safe action is   38._____

    A. face the ladder when ascending
    B. face the ladder when descending
    C. allow a maximum of 2 feet of overlap
    D. place the foot about 15 feet from the wall

39. Of the following, the type of fire extinguisher which is NEVER suitable for use on an electrical fire is   39._____

    A. liquefied gas
    C. carbon dioxide
    B. dry chemical
    D. gas cartridge actuated

40. Assume that a member of your crew has been seriously injured by an accident in the plant.
    Of the following, the FIRST thing that should be done is   40._____

    A. determine the cause of the accident
    B. order the rest of the crew back to work
    C. notify your supervisor
    D. assist the injured man

KEY (CORRECT ANSWERS)

1. D	11. B, C	21. A	31. A
2. B	12. A	22. D	32. D
3. A	13. A	23. D	33. D
4. D	14. B	24. D	34. C
5. C	15. A, B	25. B	35. A
6. B	16. D	26. B	36. C
7. D	17. C	27. C	37. A
8. D	18. B	28. A	38. C
9. C	19. C	29. B	39. A, D
10. C	20. C	30. D	40. D

EXAMINATION SECTION
TEST 1

DIRECTIONS: Each question or incomplete statement is followed by several suggested answers or completions. Select the one that BEST answers the question or completes the statement. *PRINT THE LETTEE OF THE CORRECT ANSWER IN THE SPACE AT THE RIGHT.*

1. An AC circuit consists only of a pure inductance and a power source. The relationship between the voltage and the current in this circuit is that the

    A. voltage lags the current
    B. current leads the voltage
    C. current lags the voltage
    D. voltage and current are in phase

1._____

2. The power factor of a load is equal to the _____ power divided by the _____ power.

    A. apparent; true
    B. true; apparent
    C. reactive; apparent
    D. apparent; reactive

2._____

3. A 10-ohm and a 20-ohm resistor are connected in parallel. The total line current drawn by this parallel combination is 30 amps. Under these conditions, the line voltage will be _____ volts.

    A. 150   B. 200   C. 300   D. 600

3._____

4. A 20-ohm resistor is connected in series with a parallel combination of two resistors, one of which is 10 ohms, the other 40 ohms. If the voltage across the parallel combination is 40 volts, the voltage across the 20-ohm series resistor is _____ volts.

    A. 20   B. 40   C. 80   D. 100

4._____

5. A certain 120-volt single-phase AC circuit has a power factor of 80 percent and a watt-meter reading of 1150 watts. The current drawn by the circuit is _____ amperes.

    A. 8   B. 10   C. 12   D. 14

5._____

6. If the voltage between lines of a 3-phase, 3-wire delta connected system is 2400 volts, then the phase voltage is _____ volts.

    A. 2400   B. 2080   C. 1380   D. 1200

6._____

7. A circuit consists of an inductive reactance of 15 ohms and a resistor of 20 ohms in series across a 100-volt, 60 cycle AC supply. The current in this circuit is _____ amperes.

    A. 2.9   B. 4.0   C. 5.8   D. 8.0

7._____

8. A 3-phase, 3-wire, 208-volt, 60-cycle AC service supplies a balanced load consisting of three 30-ohm resistors connected in wye. The line current under these conditions is MOST NEARLY _____ amperes.

    A. 3.5   B. 4.0   C. 6.9   D. 8.0

8._____

9. If the level of the electrolyte in a lead-acid storage battery falls below the top of the plates because of evaporation under normal operating conditions, it is BEST to add

    A. electrolyte   B. sulphuric acid
    C. hydrochloric acid   D. water

9._____

10. A 600-volt cartridge fuse must have knife blade contacts if its current rating exceeds _____ amperes.

    A. 30   B. 60   C. 80   D. 100

10._____

11. When the magnitude of the short circuit currents in a feeder circuit must be limited, this is USUALLY accomplished by means of

    A. resistors   B. reactors
    C. capacitors   D. contactors

11._____

12. The cross-sectional area in circular mils of a stranded cable having 37 strands, each of which has a diameter of 90 nils, is MOST NEARLY

    A. 81,000   B. 95,000   C. 300,000   D. 942,000

12._____

13. A coil having an average diameter of 4 inches is to be made up from a 1,260-ft.-long length of wire.
The number of turns in this coil will be MOST NEARLY

    A. 100   B. 315   C. 1,200   D. 3,780

13._____

14. The device commonly known as a *growler* is FREQUENTLY used to

    A. test DC armature windings for shorts
    B. clean commutators
    C. check insulation of circuit wiring within a raceway
    D. sound alarms

14._____

15. When a megger is applied alternately to the two leads of a direct-current electrolytic capacitor, the readings will

    A. start and remain at zero for both connections
    B. start at zero but increase gradually for one of the connections
    C. start at zero but increase gradually for both connections
    D. be high at first but decrease gradually for both connections

15._____

16. The devices used to convert direct current to alternating current are called

    A. rectifiers   B. transformers
    C. rotary converters   D. inverters

16._____

17. Of the following conditions, the one which is MOST likely to cause flashing or excessive arcing from brush to brush in a motor is

    A. brushes being set at the improper angle for the direction of rotation
    B. brush pressure being too great
    C. brushes being too hard
    D. excessively high voltage on the line

17._____

18. The currents in the armature equalizer connections in a DC generator are   18.____

    A. passed through the brushes
    B. pure DC currents
    C. DC currents containing 120 cycle ripple
    D. alternating currents

19. A generating station has one 1000-Kw and two 2000-Kw generators.   19.____
To supply 2000 Kw MOST economically, the operating conditions should be

    A. two 2000-Kw generators at half load
    B. one 2000-Kw generator at full load
    C. the 1000-Kw generator at full load and one 2000-Kw generator at half load
    D. the 1000-Kw generator at full load and each of the 2000-Kw generators at 500-Kw load

20. The terminal voltage of a DC shunt generator having an armature current of 100   20.____
amperes, an armature resistance of 0.02 ohms, and a generated E.M.F. of 222 volts is
MOST NEARLY _____ volts.

    A. 200   B. 220   C. 224   D. 242

21. The number of poles in the field of an alternator generating voltage at a frequency of 60   21.____
cycles per second while rotating at 1200 r.p.m. is

    A. 4   B. 6   C. 8   D. 12

22. If the field of a shunt motor opens while running, the motor will   22.____

    A. stop running
    B. continue to run at the same speed
    C. slow down
    D. run away

23. To reverse the direction of rotation of a cumulative compound motor, and not have it run   23.____
as a differential compound motor, reverse the connections to the _____ field.

    A. shunt   B. series
    C. shunt field and to the series   D. armature and to the shunt

24. The MAIN contributing factor to motor stator failure *usually* is   24.____

    A. eddy currents   B. bearing trouble
    C. dirt   D. hysteresis

25. The input of a motor is 40,000 watts and its efficiency is 80 percent.   25.____
The TOTAL energy loss is_____ watts.

    A. 32,000   B. 8,000   C. 5,000   D. 2,500

26. The full load current of a three-phase 5 hp motor operating at 200 volts, 60 cycles, and   26.____
having an efficiency of 80 percent and a power factor of 85 percent is MOST NEARLY
_____ amperes.

    A. 9.7   B. 12.1   C. 14.4   D. 18.0

27. Of the following motors, the one that has the BEST speed regulation is the _____ motor.   27.____

    A. series   B. compound
    C. shunt   D. split-phase

28. The full load speed of a 60-cycle, 208-volt, 3-phase induction motor having 6 poles and   28.____
operating with a slip of 10% is MOST NEARLY _____ r.p.m.

    A. 540   B. 600   C. 1080   D. 1200

29. Of the following, a MAJOR advantage of an AC synchronous motor is that it(s)   29.____

    A. does not require direct current
    B. can be used for power factor correction
    C. speed of rotation can be varied by means of a field rheostat
    D. can respond to disturbances in the power system by hunting

30. If the field current of a synchronous motor is increased to a point which makes the syn-   30.____
chronous motor overexcited, the

    A. power factor will be decreased
    B. motor rotational speed will be increased
    C. motor rotational speed will be decreased
    D. motor will take a leading current

31. When transformers are to be operated in parallel, it is NOT necessary that the trans-   31.____
former have the same

    A. ratio of transformation
    B. voltage rating
    C. polarity of the terminals that connect together
    D. KVA rating

32. A transformer rated at 200 KVA is FULLY loaded with a lagging power factor of 80%   32.____
when it is supplying

    A. 160 KW   B. 200 KW   C. 250 KVA   D. 80 KVA

33. If the current in the primary of a current transformer is 500 amperes and the transformer   33.____
has a ratio of 100 to 5, an ammeter connected to the secondary will read MOST NEARLY
_____ amperes.

    A. 5   B. 20   C. 25   D. 100

34. Assume that a switchboard ammeter which is connected to a current transformer is dam-   34.____
aged and must be removed without interrupting the service.
Of the following, an ESSENTIAL precaution to be taken before disconnecting the
ammeter is to

    A. ground the mid-point of the transformer secondary
    B. ground one end of the transformer secondary
    C. disconnect both ammeter leads simultaneously
    D. short the secondary of the transformer

35. A DC relay is rated at 6 volts and 120 ohms.
This relay can be operated from a 120 volt line by connecting a _____ -ohm resistance in _____ with the relay.

    A. 2280; parallel   B. 2280; series
    C. 2400; parallel   D. 2400; series

35._____

36. Some relays are provided with dash-pots.
The FUNCTION of these dash-pots is to provide

    A. delayed time action   B. instantaneous time action
    C. undervoltage protection   D. overcurrent protection

36._____

37. An ammeter has a full scale deflection for a current of 0.01 amperes and an internal resistance of 20 ohms.
In order to have the ammeter read full-scale for a current of 10 amperes and not damage its movement, a shunt should be used having a value of _____ ohms.

    A. 10   B. 0.2   C. 0.02   D. 0.01

37._____

38. An air circuit breaker has contacts that flash. The MOST probable cause of this trouble is that the

    A. overload relays are set too low
    B. contacts are overheating
    C. closing-coil circuit is defective
    D. barriers are broken

38._____

39. The MAIN purpose of a *shunt trip* on a circuit breaker is to

    A. open all phases in a polyphase circuit if there is a failure in any one of the phases
    B. prevent phase reversal
    C. permit the breaker to be opened electrically from a remote location, regardless of load conditions at the breaker
    D. prevent manual tripping

39._____

40. The grid-controlled gas-type electronic tube MOST often used in motor control circuits is the

    A. magnetron   B. thyratron
    C. ignitron   D. strobatron

40._____

KEY (CORRECT ANSWERS)

1.	C	11.	B	21.	B	31.	D
2.	B	12.	C	22.	D	32.	A
3.	B	13.	C	23.	C	33.	C
4.	D	14.	A	24.	C	34.	D
5.	C	15.	B	25.	B	35.	B
6.	A	16.	D	26.	C	36.	A
7.	B	17.	D	27.	C	37.	C
8.	C	18.	D	28.	C	38.	D
9.	D	19.	B	29.	B	39.	C
10.	B	20.	B	30.	D	40.	B

TEST 2

DIRECTIONS: Each question or incomplete statement is followed by several suggested answers or completions. Select the one that BEST answers the question or completes the statement. *PRINT THE LETTER OF THE CORRECT ANSWER IN THE SPACE AT THE RIGHT.*

1. Under normal atmospheric conditions, a pressure gauge that reads 24 inches of mercury is indicating an *absolute pressure* of MOST NEARLY _____ P.S.I.

    A. 26.5   B. 14.7   C. 11.8   D. 8.7

1.____

2. The PRIMARY function of a hygrometer is to measure

    A. relative humidity   B. specific gravity
    C. liquid levels   D. pressure differentials

2.____

3. A venturi meter is used to measure the rate of

    A. vibration of engine footings
    B. electric power consumption
    C. heat transfer
    D. fluid flow

3.____

4. The PRINCIPAL thickening agent used in lubricating greases is

    A. metallic soap   B. olein
    C. palmitin   D. lecithin

4.____

5. The specific gravity of liquids is USUALLY determined by means of a

    A. bolometer   B. calorimeter
    C. fathometer   D. hydrometer

5.____

6. The pull required on the fall line (neglecting friction) to hoist a 120-pound weight, using a four-part block and tackle, is _____ lbs.

    A. 30   B. 60   C. 80   D. 100

6.____

7. Of the following terms, the one which does NOT describe a way of finishing the ends of a rope is the

    A. eye splice   B. backlash
    C. whip   D. bight

7.____

8. When hoisting a load by means of a sling, the stress in each leg of the sling will

    A. increase as the angle between the horizontal and the sling leg decreases
    B. decrease as the angle between the horizontal and the sling leg decreases
    C. increase as the angle between the horizontal and the sling leg increases
    D. be independent of the angle between the horizontal and the sling leg

8.____

9. The MAXIMUM pressure in an upright cylinder 6 feet in diameter, 8 feet high, and open at the top, when filled to the brim with water, is MOST NEARLY _____ lbs/sq.ft.

    A. 250   B. 375   C. 500   D. 750

9.____

10. The MAXIMUM height to which water can be lifted by means of suction alone, at sea level, is APPROXIMATELY _____ feet. 10._____

    A. 10   B. 22   C. 34   D. 47

11. The TOTAL number of 4-inch diameter pipes that is required to equal the water flow capacity of an 8-inch diarieter pipe (neglecting friction) is 11._____

    A. 2   B. 3   C. 4   D. 5

12. The number of threads, per inch, on the standard machine screw MOST suitable for general use is 12._____

    A. 50   B. 32   C. 17   D. 10

13. The friction losses which occur when water flows through a pipe vary MOST NEARLY _____ with the _____ . 13._____

    A. *directly*; velocity squared
    B. *inversely*; velocity squared
    C. *directly*; velocity
    D. *inversely*; velocity

14. Small by-pass lines are sometimes furnished around large gate valves MAINLY to 14._____

    A. balance the pressure on the gate when the valve is being opened
    B. permit dumping of the excess fluid
    C. meter the flow
    D. divert fluid in case the valve becomes stuck

15. The sudden surge caused by an abrupt change in the speed of the pumps in a closed liquid piping system is USUALLY called 15._____

    A. tailing   B. water hammer
    C. precipitation   D. jetting

16. The valve that permits water to flow in one direction only is the _____ valve. 16._____

    A. gate   B. globe   C. angle   D. check

17. Most flanged butterfly valves can be brought from a fully closed position to a fully opened position in _____ turn(s). 17._____

    A. two full   B. one full
    C. a half   D. a quarter

18. The efficiency of two centrifugal pumps operating in parallel is _____ of one of the pumps operating alone. 18._____

    A. one-half that
    B. practically the same as that
    C. twice that
    D. four times that

19. Assume that a spur gear having 20 teeth revolves at 80 r.p.m. and drives another spur gear having 40 teeth. The speed at which the gear having 40 teeth revolves is _____ r.p.m.

    A. 160   B. 40   C. 20   D. 10

19._____

20. A centrifugal pump has a plain flat-joint seal between the impeller and the casing. If the clearance of the seal becomes enlarged due to wear, thereby reducing the pump's efficiency, it would be GOOD practice to

    A. tighten down on the casing
    B. use the pumps only in an emergency
    C. replace the wearing ring
    D. renew the impeller

20._____

21. The one of the following statements which CORRECTLY describes a speed characteristic for a centrifugal pump under normal operating conditions is:

    A. Capacity varies directly with the square of the speed
    B. Total head varies directly with the square of the speed
    C. Fluid power varies directly with the square of the speed
    D. Fluid power varies directly with the speed

21._____

22. The MAIN function of a pump stuffing box is to

    A. protect the pump against leakage at the point where the shaft passes through the pump casing
    B. provide a ball bearing race
    C. couple the pump to its motor
    D. prime the pump

22._____

23. The PROPER order of the events that take place in a 4-stroke internal combustion engine is:

    A. Air intake, power expansion, compression, and exhaust
    B. Power expansion, air intake, compression, and exhaust
    C. Air intake, compression, power expansion, and exhaust
    D.

23._____

24. The number of cycles in an internal combustion engine is AT LEAST _____ cycles.

    A. two   B. three   C. four   D. five

24._____

25. The lumens per watt taken by a lamp varies with the type and size of lamp. Given that a one candlepower light source emits 12.57 lumens, the lumens per watt taken by a 75 candlepower lamp drawing 40 watts is APPROXIMATELY

    A. 1.9   B. 6.7   C. 23.6   D. 240

25._____

26. A 230-volt, 25-cycle magnetic brake coil is to be rewound to operate properly on 60 cycles at the same voltage. Assuming that the coil at 25-cycles has 1800 turns, at 60 cycles the number of turns should be

    A. reduced to 750   B. increased to 2400
    C. reduced to 420   D. increased to 3000

26._____

27. Nichrome wire having a resistance of 200 ohms per 100 feet is to be used for a heater requiring a total resistance of 10 ohms.
The length, in feet, of wire required is
27.____

    A. 5   B. 15   C. 25   D. 50

28. The MAIN reason for grounding conduit is to prevent the conduit from becoming
28.____

    A. corroded by electrolysis
    B. magnetized
    C. a source of radio interference
    D. accidentally energized at a higher potential than ground

29. A feeder consisting of a positive and a negative wire supplies a motor load. The feeder is connected to bus-bars having a constant potential of 230 volts. The feeder is 500 ft. long and consists of two 250,000 circular-mil conductors. The maximum load on the feeder is 170 amps. Assume that the resistance of 1000 ft. of this cable is 0.0431 ohm.
The voltage, at the motor terminals, is MOST NEARLY
29.____

    A. 201V   B. 209V   C. 213V   D. 217V

30. With reference to Question 29, the efficiency of transmission, in percent, is MOST NEARLY
30.____

    A. 83%   B. 87%   C. 91%   D. 97%

31. With reference to AC motors, in addition to overload, many other things cause fuses to blow.
The fuse will blow if, in starting an AC motor, the operator throws the starting switch of the compensator to the running position
31.____

    A. too slowly
    B. too quickly
    C. with main switch in open position
    D. with main switch in closed position

32. A change in speed of a DC motor of 10 to 15 percent can USUALLY be made by
32.____

    A. rewinding the armature
    B. rewinding the field
    C. decreasing the number of turns in the field coils
    D. increasing or decreasing the gap between the armature and field

33. Of the following types of fire extinguishers, the one MOST suitable for use on fires in electrical equipment is the _____ extinguisher.
33.____

    A. soda-acid   B. loaded stream
    C. foam   D. dry chemical

34. Portable fire extinguishers suitable for use on electrical fires are USUALLY identified by a label with the following symbol_____ in a _____.
34.____

    A. *A*; triangle   B. *B*; square
    C. *C*; circle   D. *D*; five-pointed star

35. When flammable liquids are poured from one container to another, a bond wire is some-times connected between the containers to   35.____

    A. prevent the liquid from spilling
    B. prevent the containers from dropping
    C. ensure that the containers will be sealed after pouring is completed
    D. eliminate sparks due to static electricity

36. The proper way to lift a heavy object includes all of the following techniques EXCEPT   36.____

    A. placing the feet as far away from the object as possible
    B. bending the knees
    C. keeping the back straight
    D. lifting with the arm and leg muscles

37. The contents of different piping systems are sometimes identified by means of standard color codes, such as the one recommended by the American National Standards Institute (formerly the American Standards Institute). According to this Institute's standards, a piping system used for fire protection should be designated by the color   37.____

    A. green   B. blue   C. red   D. yellow

38. Assume that the contents of a container are described as *TOXIC*.
This means they are   38.____

    A. explosive   B. fragile
    C. poisonous   D. volatile

39. An authoritative source of emergency information on antidotes is the   39.____

    A. Fire Department
    B. Poison Control Center, Department of Health
    C. public library
    D. National Labor Relations Board

40. Unexpected operation of electrical equipment that can be started by remote control may cause injury to workers making repairs.
Before making repairs on such equipment, it is GOOD practice to   40.____

    A. follow a lockout procedure
    B. bypass the interlocks
    C. ground all live conductors
    D. uncouple all motors

KEY (CORRECT ANSWERS)

1.	A	11.	C	21.	B	31.	B
2.	A	12.	B	22.	A	32.	D
3.	D	13.	A	23.	C	33.	D
4.	A	14.	A	24.	A	34.	C
5.	D	15.	B	25.	C	35.	D
6.	A	16.	D	26.	A	36.	A
7.	D	17.	D	27.	D	37.	C
8.	A	18.	B	28.	D	38.	C
9.	C	19.	B	29.	D	39.	B
10.	C	20.	D	30.	D	40.	A

EXAMINATION SECTION
TEST 1

DIRECTIONS: Each question or incomplete statement is followed by several suggested answers or completions. Select the one that BEST answers the question or completes the statement. PRINT THE LETTER OF THE CORRECT ANSWER IN THE SPACE AT THE RIGHT.

1. Assume that an engine has a no-load speed of 1800 RPM and a full-load speed of 1650 RPM,
   The speed regulation of this engine is MOST NEARLY

   A. 12%.   B. 11%   C. 9.1%   D. 8.4%

1____

2. The color of the third wire used for grounding portable electric power tools is generally

   A. black   B. white   C. red   D. green

2____

3. A series circuit consists of a pure inductance and a pure resistance. When an AC voltage is impressed across such a circuit, the _____ the resistence by 90 degrees.

   A. current in the inductance lags the current in
   B. current in the inductance leads the current in
   C. voltage across the inductance lags the voltage across
   D. voltage across the inductance leads the voltage across

3____

4. Of the following devices, the one which should be used for throttling of water going through it is the _____ valve.

   A. gate   B. globe   C. check   D. relief

4____

5. If the line-to-line voltage of a wye-connected 3-phase system is 220 volts AC and the phase current is 10 amperes, then the total power delivered is MOST NEARLY _____ watts.

   A. 1270   B. 2200   C. 3800   D. 6600

5____

6. The sensitivity of a meter movement is given as 50 microamperes. This is equivalent to a voltmeter rating of _____ ohms/volt.

   A. 50,000   B. 20,000   C. 50   D. 20

6____

7. Doubling the number of turns of an inductor should _____ its original value.

   A. *reduce* the inductance to one-quarter of
   B. *reduce* the inductance to one-half of
   C. *increase* the inductance to twice
   D. *increase* the inductance to four times

7____

8. Electrical fuses are rated in

   A. current and voltage   B. current and wattage
   C. ampere-hours   D. watt-hours

8____

9. A 30-ohm resistor is placed in parallel with an inductor that has an inductive reactance of 40 ohms. If 120 volts AC is impressed across the parallel combination, the *total current* drawn from the 120-volt AC line is _____ amps.

    A. 1.7   B. 2.4   C. 3.0   D. 5.0

9____

10. The symbol shown at the right, found in the schematic of a motor control circuit represents a

    A. silicon-controlled rectifier
    B. thyratron
    C. heat-sunk diode
    D. thermal overload

10____

11. A device that can be used to check the condition of the electrolyte in a storage battery is the

    A. hygrometer   B. hydrometer
    C. hydrostat   D. aquastat

11____

12. Of the following, the BEST device to use to check the condition of the insulation of a cable is the

    A. ohmmeter   B. wheatstone bridge
    C. voltmeter   D. megger

12____

13. The decibel is a unit used in measuring the level of

    A. magnetization   B. acidity
    C. sound   D. contamination

13____

14. A rectangular bus bar with a cross-section of .1.0 inch x .50 inch has a cross-sectional area MOST NEARLY equivalent to _____ circular mils.

    A. 250,000   B. 640,000
    C. 1,000,000   D. 1,280,000

14____

15. The electrical conductivity of copper is lower than that of

    A. silver   B. gold   C. carbon   D. aluminum

15____

16. A voltmeter has a ground connection and two terminals, one of which is used for 0-300 volts and the other for 0-750 volts. The scale is marked only for the 0-750 range.
A scale reading of 200, when the 0-300 volt range is being used, corresponds to an actual voltage of _____ volts.

    A. 200   B. 160   C. 120   D. 80

16____

17. When putting out a fire with a hand extinguisher, it is BEST to direct the discharge at the _____ the fire.

    A. base of   B. area behind
    C. area in front of   D. highest flames of

17____

18. Someone suggests that the silver-plated main contacts of a circuit breaker be cleaned with fine sandpaper. This suggestion is   18____

   A. *poor,* since the useful silver plating would be removed
   B. *good,* since you would be removing silver oxide which is a poor conductor
   C. *good,* since this will prevent overheating of the circuit breaker
   D. *poor,* since this will change the adjustment of the main contacts

19. If a multi-scale DC voltmeter reads downscale (goes below zero) when connected across two pins of an electrical connector, it is MOST likely that the   19____

   A. meter is defective
   B. voltage across the pins is AC
   C. meter leads are reversed
   D. wrong scale is being used

20. Measurements of illumination in a work area are made with light meters which measure in units of   20____

   A. foot-lamberts   B. foot-candles
   C. lumens   D. watts

21. Assume that new types of circuit breakers and controls are to be installed in the plant where you work. This equipment is to be operated and maintained by you. Of the following, the FIRST step you should take to become familiar with the new equipment is to   21____

   A. read the instruction books for the equipment
   B. call in the manufacturer's field personnel for instructions
   C. read textbooks on the general theory of such equipment
   D. make trial disassemblies and reassemblies of the equipment

22. Of the following, the BEST way to lift a heavy object is to   22____

   A. keep legs spread apart and straight, slowly bending at the waist to grasp the object
   B. place the feet about shoulder-width apart and slowly bend at the knees to reach down to the object
   C. keep legs straight and close together, slowly bending at the waist to grasp the object
   D. place feet close together, and with legs and back straight, bend at the waist to reach down and quickly lift the object

23. Sparks and open flames should be kept away from storage batteries that are being charged because of the high combustibility of the   23____

   A. electrolytes in the batteries
   B. battery cases when hot
   C. gases being produced
   D. sulfuric acid fumes being generated

24. A 16-foot wood ladder is to be leaned against a wall. Of the following, the SAFEST distance at which the base of the ladder should be placed from the base of the wall is _____ feet.   24____

   A. 4   B. 6   C. 8   D. 9

25. Of the following fittings, the one used to connect two lengths of conduit in a straight line is a(n)   25____

    A. elbow   B. nipple   C. tee   D. coupling

26. If a nut is to be tightened to an exact specified value, the wrench that should be used is a(n) _____ wrench.   26____

    A. torque   B. lock-j aw   C. alligator   D. spanner

27. Unloaders are generally found on   27____

    A. centrifugal pumps   B. air compressors
    C. flexible couplings   D. surge suppressors

28. A compound gauge indicates   28____

    A. pressures in lbs. and vacuums in inches of water
    B. both pressures and vacuums in lbs. per sq. inch
    C. pressures in lbs. per sq. inch and vacuums in inches of mercury
    D. pressures in lbs. and vacuums in inches of mercury per sq. inch

29. Of the following, the metal that is used for bearing linings is   29____

    A. Muntz metal   B. duraluminum
    C. naval brass   D. babbitt

30. It has been discovered that the commutator of an electrical machine has developed a flat spot.   30____
    To remove the flat spot, the

    A. entire commutator should be ground or turned down until the flat spot is removed
    B. brushes should be changed to a harder grade and the flat spot will eventually wear away
    C. entire commutator should be resurfaced with emery cloth attached to a wooden block which is then pressed against the turning commutator
    D. commutator bars that have the flat spot should be removed for repair or replace-ment, then reassembled back into the commutator

31. The FIRST operation performed on raw sewage as it comes into a sewage treatment plant is to   31____

    A. add sufficient amounts of chlorine to kill any living organisms
    B. place it into settling tanks to allow sludge to settle to the bottom
    C. pass it through screens to remove or break up coarse material
    D. introduce selected bacteria to initiate biodegrada-tion

32. The MAIN function of diffusers in sewage treatment plants is to   32____

    A. maintain a uniform distribution of non-solubles in the sewage
    B. release compressed air into the sewage
    C. pass the sewage through a fine filter
    D. disperse objectionable and toxic gases that are formed in the sewage

33. A comminutor at a sewage plant is used to   33____

    A. shred sewage matter that is not removed by screens
    B. enable people in one building to talk to people in other buildings
    C. convert AC electric power to DC in the sewage plant
    D. reduce the level of noise in the sewage settling basin building

34. The pH of a substance is an indication of its   34____

    A. resistance to corrosion
    B. magnetic properties
    C. transparency or translucency
    D. acidity or alkalinity

35. Assume that a vacuum gauge reads 15 inches of Hg. The equivalent in *absolute pressure* is MOST NEARLY _____ p.s.i.   35____

    A. 2.0   B. 4.0   C. 7.5   D. 14.7

KEY (CORRECT ANSWERS)

1.	C		16.	D
2.	D		17.	A
3.	D		18.	A
4.	B		19.	C
5.	C		20.	B
6.	B		21.	A
7.	D		22.	B
8.	A		23.	C
9.	D		24.	A
10.	A		25.	D
11.	B		26.	A
12.	D		27.	B
13.	C		28.	C
14.	B		29.	D
15.	A		30.	A

31.	C
32.	B
33.	A
34.	D
35.	C

TEST 2

DIRECTIONS: Each question or incomplete statement is followed by several suggested answers or completions. Select the one that BEST answers the question or completes the statement. *PRINT THE LETTER OF THE CORRECT ANSWER IN THE SPACE AT THE RIGHT.*

1. An ADVANTAGE of a rotary pump over a centrifugal pump is that the rotary pump is   1____

    A.   self-priming and requires no valves
    B.   better able to handle gritty water
    C.   better suited for high pressures and high discharges
    D.   quieter and has a pulseless discharge

2. A method used to eliminate water hammer in a water line is to   2____

    A.   increase the pressure in the line
    B.   use slow-closing valves and faucets
    C.   treat the water with a water softener
    D.   increase the temperature of the water

3. A pipe nipple that is threaded over its entire length is called a _____ nipple.   3____

    A.   shoulder   B.   long   C.   close   D.   short

4. A Stillson wrench is also called a _____ wrench.   4____

    A.   strap   B.   pipe   C.   monkey   D.   crescent

5. In a piping diagram, the symbol shown at the right represents a   5____

    A.   pressure regulator   B.   strainer
    C.   check valve   D.   drier

6. A shut-off valve is found to have the designation *WOG 300*. The letters WOG mean   6____

    A.   Water or Gas Valve
    B.   Water, Oil or Gas Pressure
    C.   Worthington Gate Valve
    D.   Working Gauge Pressure

7. A plunger-type compressed-air-driven reciprocating water pump has a marking *3x4x7*.   7____
    The number *7* refers to the

    A.   diameter of the compressed air piston in inches
    B.   diameter of the water piston in inches
    C.   length of the stroke in inches
    D.   compression ratio

8. Methane is a gas that   8____

    A.   has a smell like rotten eggs
    B.   is heavier than air
    C.   forms the major part of natural gas
    D.   is non-combustible

9. As a cylinder in a diesel engine is going through its compression cycle, the air in the cylinder will _____ in pressure and _____ in temperature.

   A. *decrease; decrease*   B. *increase; increase*
   C. decrease; increase   D. *increase; decrease*

10. A specification for the installation of a storage tank indicates that a hydrostatic test
    should be made before placing the tank in service.
    A hydrostatic test consists of

    A. immersing the tank, with ports closed, in water and checking for water seeping in
    B. filling the tank with water under pressure and noting how well the pressure is held
       or whether water leaks out
    C. creating a vacuum in the interior of the tank and noting how well the vacuum is held
       or whether air leaks in
    D. filling the tank with compressed air and checking for leaks with soapy water

11. When the ignition characteristics of a fuel are represented by a cetane number, the fuel
    is one that is normally used in a

    A. gasoline engine   B. gas turbine
    C. diesel engine   D. steam boiler

12. Of the following, a characteristic of a wound-rotor AC induction motor is that it

    A. provides a wide range of speed control
    B. does not require slip-rings
    C. has a *squirrel cage* armature
    D. operates on single-phase power

13. Detergents are used in lubricating oils to

    A. reduce the S.A.E. number
    B. prevent oxidation of the oil
    C. keep insoluble matter in suspension
    D. combat corrosion

14. In a four-stroke diesel engine, each piston fires every _____ of the crankshaft.

    A. one-half revolution   B. revolution
    C. two revolutions   D. four revolutions

15. An electric motor with pressure grease fittings and relief plugs requires lubrication,
    A grease gun should be connected to each fitting and the grease gun should be
    pumped *until*

    A. grease oozes out along the shaft
    B. grease oozes out from the relief plug hole
    C. the handle becomes hard to move
    D. the handle starts to move freely

16. Of the following, the one which is NOT used for applying grease to a bearing is a(n)

    A. Alemite fitting   B. grease cup
    C. Zerk fitting   D. pressure plug

17. Of the following, the substance that should be used to melt ice on pavements and walk-   17____
ways is called

    A. calcium chloride   B. trichloroethylene
    C. sodium hydroxide   D. slaked lime

18. On a working drawing, the symbol (shading) given as shown at the   18____
right represents

    A. cast iron   B. concrete   C. glass   D. steel

19. A machine screw is indicated on a drawing as The head is the   19____
American Standard type called _____ head.

    A. flat   B. oval   C. fillister   D. round

20. The tool that is shown at the right is properly referred to as   20____
a(n) _____ tap.

    A. bottoming   B. acme   C. taper   D. plug

21. The tool indicated at the right is referred to as an   21____
arch punch.
This tool should be used to

    A. cut holes in 1/16 inch steel
    B. cut large diameter holes in masonry
    C. run through a conduit prior to pulling a cable or wires
    D. make holes in rubber or leather gasket material

22. Before putting an aerosol container for garbage pickup, it is *good* practice to   22____

    A. puncture it with a screwdriver
    B. use out the contents in normal manner
    C. put it out as is regardless of container contents
    D. remove the spray nozzle

23. A lantern ring is a type of   23____

    A. optical illusion on a light source seen through a fine screen mesh
    B. sealing arrangement used to minimize air leakage between a rotating shaft and a
       sleeve
    C. piston ring which provides lubrication of the cylinder wall
    D. oil ring bearing lubrication

24. Monel metal is an alloy used for water heater tanks. It is a combination MAINLY of   24____

    A. iron and lead   B. chromium and zinc
    C. nickel and copper   D. vanadium and tin

25. The plumbing fitting shown at the right is called a   25____

    A. Street Elbow
    B. Return Bend
    C. Running Trap
    D. Reversing *El*

26. A galvanized steel plate is a plate with a coating of   26____

    A. lead and tin alloy   B. tin
    C. zinc   D. brass

27. *If* the barrel of a standard micrometer is rotated through one complete revolution, the *gap*   27____
dimension is changed by _____ inch,

    A. .010   B. .025   C. .100   D. .250

28. Of the following, the indication that a fluorescent lamp is in need of replacement is that   28____

    A. a very low level hum is produced by the ballast
    B. there is a slight delay before the lamp comes up to full brightness after the switch is
        turned on
    C. the lamp flashes on and off, and there are black coatings at the ends
    D. the lamp does not go off each time the switch is turned off

29. The one of the following that is recommended for prime-coating bare metals is   29____

    A. varnish   B. zinc chromate
    C. shellac   D. linseed oil

30. *Dressing* a grinding wheel refers to   30____

    A. replacing the wheel with a new one
    B. reducing the thickness of the wheel
    C. cleaning the grinding surface and making the wheel round
    D. repositioning the wheel on its shaft to eliminate *wobble*

31. A fusible metal plug is a protective device that   31____

    A. melts when the electric current through it exceeds the rating
    B. melts when its temperature reaches a specific figure
    C. ruptures when the pressure behind it goes beyond a certain level
    D. ruptures when the *pull* on it exceeds a specified number of pounds

32. Of the following, the material that is beginning to be used for electrical conduits, plastic   32____
water pipes, and electrical insulation is

    A. trichloroethyline   B. polyvinylchloride
    C. carbontrichlorofluoride   D. teflon

33. At certain conditions of speed, pressure, and temperature, centrifugal pumps can be made to cavitate.
The conditions causing cavitation

    A. should be avoided since the impeller may become seriously pitted
    B. result in the highest pump efficiency
    C. produce *water hammer* and should be avoided
    D. also produce the quietest operation of the pump

33____

34. A nut is turned on a 1/2" - 10 bolt.
When the nut is turned through five complete turns on the bolt, the distance it moves longitudinally on the bolt is _____ inch.

    A. .100   B. .200   C. .375   D. .500

34____

35. A growler is a device used for

    A. vibrating pipes carrying solid matter
    B. sounding an alarm when hazardous conditions develop
    C. detecting shorts in armatures
    D. chewing up solids in sewage

35____

KEY (CORRECT ANSWERS)

1.	A		16.	D
2.	B		17.	A
3.	C		18.	D
4.	B		19.	B
5.	C		20.	A
6.	B		21.	D
7.	C		22.	B
8.	C		23.	B
9.	B		24.	C
10.	B		25.	B
11.	C		26.	C
12.	A		27.	B
13.	C		28.	C
14.	C		29.	B
15.	B		30.	C

31.	B
32.	B
33.	A
34.	D
35.	C

EXAMINATION SECTION
TEST 1

DIRECTIONS: Each question or incomplete statement is followed by several suggested answers or completions. Select the one that BEST answers the question or completes the statement. *PRINT THE LETTER OF THE CORRECT ANSWER IN THE SPACE AT THE RIGHT.*

1. Assume that certain work assignments are not liked by any of your subordinates. As this work has to be done, you, as the stationary engineer (electric), should try as much as possible to

    A. assign this work as punishment details
    B. rotate the work assignments among subordinates
    C. assign this work to the best-natured man
    D. assign this work to the junior men

1.____

2. A stationary engineer (electric), in discussing new departmental regulations with his sub-ordinates, commented,
We should be conscious of the fact that our interests are mutual, and that by all of us in unison putting our shoulders to the wheel and working together, we can achieve our common objective. This approach is _____, because it will _____.

    A. good; promote cooperation
    B. poor; invite excessive criticism
    C. good; promote good fellowship
    D. poor; invite too much familiarity

2.____

3. In the inspection of relays, the type of trouble encountered often depends on the type of relay.
The one of the following which is NOT a trouble encountered with an induction-type relay is

    A. friction between disc and magnet
    B. dust on disc
    C. foreign matter in gear train
    D. punctured bellows

3.____

4. It is sometimes desirable to have a control that will cause a DC motor to come to a stand-still quickly instead of coasting to a standstill after the stop button is pressed.
This result is MOST commonly obtained by means of an action called

    A. counter emf method   B. armature reaction
    C. diverting   D. dynamic braking

4.____

5. In an electric circuit, a high spot temperature is MOST commonly due to

    A. an open circuit
    B. a defective connection
    C. intermittent use of circuit
    D. excessive distribution voltage

5.____

6. The MAIN reason for periodic inspections and testing of equipment in an electrically powered plant is to   6.____

    A. keep the men busy at all times
    B. familiarize the men with the equipment
    C. train the men to be ready in an emergency
    D. discover minor faults before they have a chance to become significantly serious

7. Assume that an employee calls up to give advance notice of his intentions to be absent the following day.
The MOST important information that he should give is the   7.____

    A. exact time of calling
    B. balance of his sick leave time
    C. reason for his absence
    D. name of his attending doctor

8. The MAIN reason why a stationary engineer who is assigned to service equipment must be able to make proper adjustments and repairs quickly is that   8.____

    A. equipment always deteriorates rapidly unless readjusted immediately
    B. idle equipment will result in poor plant efficiency and work delays
    C. the ability to work rapidly is the result of extensive training and experience
    D. he will have more time for his other duties

9. Assume that you see one of your oilers tumble down a long flight of concrete steps and fall heavily on the lower landing. You rush to him and find that he is unconscious but breathing.
Of the following, the BEST course of action for you to take is   9.____

    A. have two of your men carry him into the office and summon a doctor
    B. do not move him but cover him with a blanket and call a doctor
    C. prop him upright and let him inhale spirits of ammonia and call a doctor
    D. prepare a bed of blankets and have two of your men lift him on it; then summon a doctor

10. The MAIN reason that larger size electrical cables (such as #0000) are always stranded rather than solid is that they   10.____

    A. are more flexible
    B. are stronger
    C. have a higher conductivity
    D. have a higher specific resistance

11. The purpose of full wave rectifiers is to   11.____

    A. produce AC current which contains some DC
    B. change DC current to AC
    C. produce DC current having an AC ripple of twice the input frequency
    D. produce only AC current having twice the input frequency

12. The temporary production of a substitute for a two-phase current so as to obtain a make-   12.____
shift rotating field in starting a single phase motor is called

    A. phase splitting   B. pole pitch
    C. phase transformation   D. pole splitting

13. When batteries are being charged, they should NOT be exposed to open flames and   13.____
sparks because of the flammability of

    A. hydrogen   B. oxygen
    C. sulphurous gas   D. fuming sulphuric acid

14. Assume that you and your supervisor are on an inspectional tour of the outdoor equip-   14.____
ment of the plant and that a co-worker suddenly falls unconscious on the pavement.
If, on close observation, you find that the victim is not breathing, the FIRST thing to do
is

    A. move the victim indoors
    B. notify his family
    C. administer first aid to restore breathing
    D. nothing, but summon a doctor

15. Assume that one of your men, who has always been efficient, industrious, and conscien-   15.____
tious, suddenly becomes lax in his work, makes numerous mistakes, and shuns
responsibilities.
The cause of such a change

    A. is usually that the man is responding to a minor change in the job situation
    B. is usually apparent to the stationary engineer in charge and fellow workers
    C. may be quickly found by a close study of reports and personnel records
    D. may have no direct relationship to any change in the job situation

16. Circuit conductors operating at 600 volts or less may be worked upon live, without open-   16.____
ing the circuit, if certain precautionary measures are taken.
The one of the following that BEST represents one of these precautionary measures
for this work is:

    A. Bare or exposed places on one conductor must be taped after another conductor is
        first exposed
    B. Adjacent live or grounded conductors shall be covered with a conducting material
    C. Bare or exposed places on one conductor must be taped before another conductor
        is exposed
    D. Adjacent live or grounded conductors shall be securely bonded to the ground

17. In order to properly distribute the load (in proportion to their rated capacities) between   17.____
two alternators which are operating in parallel, it is necessary to

    A. overexcite the smaller alternator and underexcite the larger one
    B. adjust the governor on the prime mover
    C. underexcite the larger alternator, but use normal excitation on the smaller one
    D. underexcite the smaller alternator and overexcite the larger one

4 (#1)

18. If a large amount of flame is visible from a small pile of burning material, the material must contain a substance that   18.____

   A. contains a large amount of inorganic material
   B. produces, during the burning process, a large amount of pure carbon
   C. produces, during the burning process, a large amount of combustible gases or vapors
   D. is composed almost entirely of pure carbon

19. In the zeolite process for water treatment, calcium and magnesium are removed by   19.____

   A. absorption   B. evaporation
   C. settling   D. filtration

20. Reprimanding a subordinate for inefficiency in the presence of fellow co-workers is apt to   20.____

   A. cause the subordinate to resign
   B. arouse the subordinate's resentment
   C. improve the performance of all present
   D. cause the subordinate to improve

21. A heat exchanger commonly located between the low pressure and high pressure cylinders of an air compressor is used to _____ of the compressor air.   21.____

   A. lower the temperature
   B. increase the relative humidity
   C. decrease the relative humidity
   D. raise the temperature

22. The one of the following instruments which is used for the determination of the velocity of air in ducts is the   22.____

   A. psychrometer   B. pitot tube
   C. U gauge   D. spherometer

23. A high tension breaker (4160 volts) should be equipped with a mechanical interlock which will prevent the breaker from being raised or advanced into, and lowered or withdrawn from, the operating position UNLESS   23.____

   A. it is open
   B. it is closed
   C. the full load is connected
   D. a light load is connected

24. The proper fire extinguishing agent to use to extinguish fires in electrical equipment is   24.____

   A. water   B. foam
   C. soda-acid   D. carbon dioxide

25. Direct current motors, for best performance, should have their brushes set on the commutator   25.____

   A. at the neutral point (under load)
   B. at the point of maximum armature reaction
   C. radially at an angle of 90° (leading)
   D. radially at an angle of 80° (leading)

68

26. The PROPER order of events that take place in a 4-stroke cycle diesel engine is   26.____

    A. air intake, power expansion, compression, and exhaust
    B. air intake, compression, power, expansion, and exhaust
    C. power expansion, air intake, compression, and exhaust
    D. compression, air intake, power expansion, and exhaust

27. The one of the following lubricants which is LEAST likely to be attacked by acids is   27.____

    A. cottonseed oil   B. castor oil
    C. rapeseed oil   D. graphite

28. In general, non-rising steam gate valves are BEST adaptable for   28.____

    A. use where frequent adjustments are necessary
    B. installations carrying viscous liquids
    C. throttling or close control
    D. places where space is a factor

29. The presence of moisture in insulating oil is undesirable. The percentage of moisture which will reduce the dielectric strength of insulating oil to approximately one-half of its dielectric strength when dry is MOST NEARLY _____ % of moisture.   29.____

    A. 0.5   B. 0.05   C. 0.005   D. 0.0005

30. It has been brought to your attention that one of the men under your supervision is complaining to fellow co-workers that another man has received an easy assignment through his *connections*.
In this situation, it is BEST to   30.____

    A. privately inform the man who is complaining of the truth regarding the assignment
    B. in the presence of others, demand absolute proof from the man who is complaining
    C. ignore the matter since it is not your job to interfere in disagreements between the men
    D. tell the complaining man to apply for a desirable assignment also

KEY (CORRECT ANSWERS)

1. B	16. C
2. A	17. D
3. D	18. C
4. D	19. A
5. B	20. B
6. D	21. A
7. C	22. B
8. B	23. C
9. B	24. D
10. A	25. C
11. C	26. B
12. A	27. D
13. A	28. D
14. C	29. C
15. D	30. A

TEST 2

DIRECTIONS: Each question or incomplete statement is followed by several suggested answers or completions. Select the one that BEST answers the question or completes the statement. *PRINT THE LETTER OF THE CORRECT ANSWER IN THE SPACE AT THE RIGHT.*

1. The direction of rotation of a DC shunt motor can be reversed by reversing the   1._____

   A. line leads
   B. armature *and* field current
   C. field *or* armature current
   D. current in one pole winding

2. The insulation resistance of the stator winding of an induction motor is MOST commonly measured or tested with a(n)   2._____

   A. strobe   B. ammeter   C. megger   D. S-meter

3. Assume that three 12 ohm resistors are connected in delta across a 208 volt, 3-phase circuit.   3._____
   The line current, in amperes, will be MOST NEARLY

   A. 30   B. 20.4   C. 17.32   D. 8.66

4. Assume that three 12 ohm resistors are connected in wye across a 208 volt, 3-phase circuit.   4._____
   The power, in watts, dissipated in this resistance load will be MOST NEARLY

   A. 4200   B. 3600   C. 1200   D. 900

5. The one of the following knots which is MOST commonly used to shorten a rope without cutting it is the   5._____

   A. clove hitch   B. diamond knot
   C. sheepshank   D. square knot

6. Cast iron castings that need repairing are USUALLY repaired by the process known as   6._____

   A. electric arc welding   B. electro-forming
   C. resistance welding   D. brazing

7. The term SAE stands for   7._____

   A. Standard Auto Engines
   B. Standard Air Engines
   C. Society of Automotive Engineers
   D. Society of Aviation Engineers

8. The type of valve which is generally used where extremely close regulation of flow is needed is the _____ valve.   8._____

   A. gate   B. globe   C. needle   D. blow-off

9. Lubricating oils of mineral origin are refined from _____ products.　　　　9._____

    A.　lard-beef　　　　　　　　　　B.　cottonseed
    C.　crude petroleum　　　　　　　D.　lime soap

10. The compression ratio of a diesel engine that has no starting ignition device is GENER-　10._____
ALLY in the range of

    A.　11 to 20　　　　B.　8 to 10　　　　C.　6 to 8　　　　D.　4 to 6

11. The base in a lubricating grease denotes the　　　　　　　　　　　　　　11._____

    A.　type of soap used in its manufacture
    B.　consistency and texture of the grease
    C.　dropping or melting point of the grease
    D.　residue content of the grease

12. Of the following sets of pipes, the one having a total combined area EXACTLY equal to　12._____
the area of a 12" diameter pipe is _____ 6" pipes and _____ 8" pipes.

    A.　two; no　　　　B.　no; two　　　　C.　two; one　　　　D.　four; no

13. If rubber gloves commonly used on high tension work are found on testing to have pin-　13._____
holes, they

    A.　may be used on low voltage
    B.　should be discarded
    C.　should be patched with rubber tape
    D.　may be used only in dry places

14. Of the following types of soap-based greases, the one which has a fibrous texture is　14._____

    A.　calcium　　　　B.　sodium　　　　C.　aluminum　　　　D.　lithium

15. Of the following types of soap-based greases, the one that is BEST for lubricating plain　15._____
bearings and line shafting is

    A.　calcium　　　　B.　sodium　　　　C.　aluminum　　　　D.　lithium

16. One of the difficult features of steam turbine lubrication is　　　　　　　　16._____

    A.　extreme oil pressure required
    B.　emulsification of the oil
    C.　excessive acidity or alkalinity of available oils
    D.　limitation on the size of oil coolers

17. The rate of oil feed to a steam engine is USUALLY specified in　　　　　　17._____

    A.　saybolt universal seconds
    B.　capacity per running time
    C.　pints per hour
    D.　drops per minute

18. The grade of oil GENERALLY used to lubricate a worm gear is SAE　　　　18._____

    A.　20　　　　B.　30　　　　C.　50　　　　D.　140

19. The distinguishing characteristic of steam-engine cylinder oil is 19.____

    A. a high flash point   B. a low flash point
    C. its color   D. its oiliness

20. Degrees Baume is a measure of fuel oil 20.____

    A. temperature   B. viscosity
    C. density   D. flash and fire point

21. How does cylinder oil compare with engine oil at room temperature? 21.____
Cylinder oil

    A. is lighter in color
    B. has a higher viscosity
    C. has a lower viscosity
    D. is lighter when put in front of a light

22. For the operation of a high tension breaker (4160 volts), the suitable control voltage for 22.____
BEST performance is

    A. 600 volts AC   B. 600 volts DC
    C. 208 to 440 volts AC   D. 70 to 140 volts DC

23. The equipment on which you would be MOST likely to find an unloader is a(n) 23.____

    A. centrifugal water pump   B. air compressor
    C. vacuum pump   D. steam engine

24. The term Saybolt refers to a measure of 24.____

    A. specific gravity   B. boiling point
    C. hardness   D. viscosity

25. Assume that a centrifugal fan running at 750 rpm delivers 20,000 cfm at a static pressure 25.____
of one inch.
If this fan is required to deliver 28,000 cfm at the same static pressure, it should be run
at a speed, in rpm, of MOST NEARLY

    A. 1500   B. 1250   C. 1150   D. 1050

26. The horsepower of a fan varies as the _____ of the fan speed. 26.____

    A. cube   B. square
    C. square root   D. cube root

27. The gearing for transmitting power between two shafts at right angles to each other con- 27.____
sists of two essential parts:

    A. two worm wheels   B. a worm and bevel gear
    C. a rack and pinion   D. two bevel gears

28. If a transmission main drive gear, having 30 teeth, rotates at 400 rpm and drives a coun- 28.____
tershaft drive gear at 300 rpm, the total number of teeth on the countershaft drive gear
will be

    A. 30   B. 40   C. 60   D. 80

29. The one of the following faults of a circuit breaker main contact which is NOT a cause of overheating of air circuit breakers is   29.____

    A. excessive pressure
    B. insufficient area in contact
    C. oxidized contacts
    D. dirty contacts

30. Of the following ranges of oil viscosities, the range MOST suitable for the lubrication of both cylinders and bearings of a reciprocating water cooled compressor, in Saybolt Universal seconds at 100° F is   30.____

    A. 10-110   B. 100-200   C. 300-400   D. 600-700

KEY (CORRECT ANSWERS)

1.	A		16.	B
2.	C		17.	D
3.	C		18.	C
4.	B		19.	A
5.	C		20.	C
6.	D		21.	B
7.	C		22.	D
8.	C		23.	B
9.	C		24.	D
10.	A		25.	D
11.	C		26.	A
12.	D		27.	D
13.	B		28.	B
14.	B		29.	A
15.	A		30.	B

Section I. COMMON MARKINGS AND SYMBOLS USED ON ELECTRICAL CIRCUIT DIAGRAMS

C-1. Common Markings to Designate Functions

Common markings are used on electrical circuit diagrams to designate the functional use of a device. Table C-1 gives a list of markings most frequently used.

Table C-1. Common Markings Used to Designate Functions

Device	Contractor designation	Relay designation	Other equipment designation
Accelerating	A	AR	
Ammeter switch			AS
Autotransformer			AT
Brake	B	BR	
Capacitor			C
Circuit breaker			CB
Closing coil		CCR	CC
Control		CR	
Control switch			CS
Counter EMF		CEMF	
Current limit		CLR	
Current transformer			CT
Down	D		
Dynamic braking	DB	DBR	
Emergency switch			ES
Exciter field	EF	EFR	
Field	F	FR	
Field accelerating	FA	FAR	
Field discharge	FD	FDR	
Field economy	FE	FER	
Field loss (failure)	FL	FLR	
Field weakening	FW	FWR	
Float flow switch			FS
Forward	F	FR	
Full field	FF	FFR	
Ground detector			GD
High speed	HS	HSR	
Hoist	H	HR	
Jam, jog	J	JR	
Kickoff	KO	KOR	
Limit switch			LS
Lowering	L	LR	
Low speed	LS	LSR	
Main breaker			MB
Master switch			MS
Motor circuit switch			MCS

Table C-1. Common Markings Used to Designate Functions—Continued

Device	Contractor designation	Relay designation	Other equipment designation
Motor field			MF
Overload		OL	
Oversupeed		OSR	
Overspeed switch			OSS
Plugging	P	PR	
Plugging forward		PF	
Plugging reverse		PR	
Potential transformer			PT
Power factor		PFR	
Power factor meter			PF
Pushbutton			PB
Rectifier			REC
Resistor			RES
Reverse, run. raise	R		
Sequence protective		SPR	
Slow down		SR	
Squirrel-cage protective.		SCR	
Start	S		
Switch			SW
Time closing			TC
Time opening			TO
Time relay		TR	
Transfer relay		TRR	
Trip coil			TC
Undervoltage	UV	UVR	
Up	U		
Voltage regulator		VRG	
Voltmeter switch			VS

C-2. Power-Terminal Markings

Common markings for designating power terminals on electrical circuit diagrams consist of a capital letter followed by a suffix numeral. If a multiplicity of equal devices are used, they are further designated by a numeral followed by a letter. Thus, 1A and 2A are device designations. A_1 and A_2 are terminal markings. Table C-2 gives a partial list of terminal markings.

Table C-2. Power-Terminal Markings

	Direct current	Alternating current
Brake	B1, B2, B3	B1, B2, B3.
Brush on commutator (armature).	A1, A2	A1, A2, A3.
Brush on slipring (rotor)		M1, M2, M3.
Field (series)	S1, S2	
Field (shunt)	F1, F2	F1, F2.
Line	L1, L2	L1, L2, L3.
Resistance (armature)	R1, R2, R3	R1, R2, R3.
Resistance (shunt field)	V1, V2, V3	
Stator		T1, T2, T3.
Transformer (high voltage).		H1, H2, H3.
Transformer (low voltage).		X1, X2, X3.

C-3. Symbols

It is common practice to use symbols to designate various pieces of equipment and everyone recognizes the equipment represented by the symbols, although there may be no resemblance between the symbol and the physical appearance of the article represented. Figure C-1 shows a list of symbols generally used in electrical circuit diagrams.

NAME	SYMBOL
BATTERY	
CAPACITOR, FIXED	
CIRCUIT BREAKERS	
AIR CIRCUIT BREAKER	
THREE-POLE POWER CIRCUIT BREAKER (SINGLE THROW) (WITH TERMINALS)	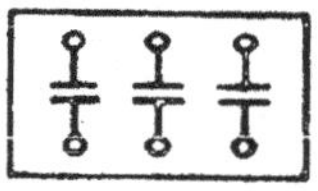
THERMAL TRIP AIR CIRCUIT BREAKER	
COILS	
NON-MAGNETIC CORE-FIXED	
MAGNETIC CORE-FIXED	
MAGNETIC CORE-ADJUSTABLE TAP OR SLIDE WIRE	
OPERATING COIL	
BLOWOUT COIL	
BLOWOUT COIL WITH TERMINALS	
SERIES FIELD	
SHUNT FIELD	
COMMUTATING FIELD	

Figure C-1. Symbols of American Standards Association (1 of 5).

NAME	SYMBOL

CONNECTIONS (MECHANICAL)

MECHANICAL CONNECTION OF SHIELD

MECHANICAL INTERLOCK

DIRECT CONNECTED UNITS

CONNECTIONS (WIRING)

ELECTRIC CONDUCTOR—CONTROL

ELECTRIC CONDUCTOR—POWER

JUNCTION OF CONDUCTORS

WIRING TERMINAL

GROUND

CROSSING OF CONDUCTORS — NOT
CONNECTED

CROSSING OF CONNECTED CONDUCTORS

JOINING OF CONDUCTORS — NOT CROSSING

CONTACTS (ELECTRICAL)

NORMALLY CLOSED CONTACT (NC)

NORMALLY OPEN CONTACT (NO)

NO CONTACT WITH TIME CLOSING (TC)
FEATURE

NC CONTACT WITH TIME OPENING (TO)
FEATURE

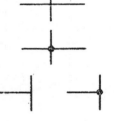

NOTE: NO (NORMALLY OPEN) AND NC
(NORMALLY CLOSED) DESIGNATES
THE POSITION OF THE CONTACTS
WHEN THE MAIN DEVICE IS IN
THE DE-ENERGIZED OR NONOPER-
ATED POSITION.

Figure C-1—Continued—(2 of 5).

NAME	SYMBOL

CONTACTOR, SINGLE-POLE, ELECTRICALLY
OPERATED, WITH BLOWOUT COIL

    NOTE: FUNDAMENTAL SYMBOLS FOR CONTACTS,
        COILS, MECHANICAL CONNECTIONS, etc.,
        ARE THE BASIS OF CONTACTOR SYMBOLS

FUSE

INDICATING LIGHTS

    INDICATING LAMP WITH LEADS

    INDICATING LAMP WITH TERMINALS

INSTRUMENTS

    AMMETER, WITH TERMINALS

 OR

    VOLTMETER, WITH TERMINALS

 OR

    WATTMETER, WITH TERMINALS

 OR

MACHINES (ROTATING)

    MACHINE OR ROTATING ARMATURE

    SQUIRREL- CAGE INDUCTION MOTOR

    WOUND-ROTOR INDUCTION MOTOR
    OR GENERATOR

    SYNCHRONOUS MOTOR, GENERATOR
    OR CONDENSER

    D-C COMPOUND MOTOR OR GENERATOR

    NOTE: COMMUTATING, SERIES, AND SHUNT
        FIELDS MAY BE INDICATED BY
        1, 2 AND 3 ZIGZAGS RESPECTIVELY.
        SERIES AND SHUNT COILS MAY BE
        INDICATED BY HEAVY AND LIGHT
        LINES OR 1 AND 2 ZIGZAGS RE-
        SPECTIVELY.

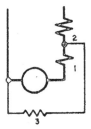

Figure C–1—Continued—(3 of 5).

NAME	SYMBOL

WINDING SYMBOLS

    THREE PHASE WYE (UNGROUNDED)

    THREE PHASE WYE (GROUNDED)

    THREE PHASE DELTA

    NOTE: WINDING SYMBOLS MAY BE SHOWN
           IN CIRCLES FOR ALL MOTOR AND
           GENERATOR SYMBOLS.

**RECTIFIER, DRY OR ELECTROLYTIC,
FULL WAVE**

FULL WAVE

RELAYS

    OVERCURRENT OR OVERVOLTAGE RELAY
    WITH 1 NO CONTACT   OR

    THERMAL OVERLOAD RELAY HAVING
    2 SERIES HEATING ELEMENTS AND
    1 NC CONTACT   OR

RESISTORS

    RESISTOR, FIXED, WITH LEADS

    RESISTOR, FIXED, WITH TERMINALS

    RESISTOR, ADJUSTABLE TAP OR
    SLIDE WIRE

    RESISTOR, ADJUSTABLE BY FIXED LEADS

    RESISTOR, ADJUSTABLE BY FIXED
    TERMINALS

    INSTRUMENT OR RELAY SHUNT

SWITCHES

    KNIFE SWITCH, SINGLE-POLE (SP)

    KNIFE SWITCH, DOUBLE-POLE SINGLE-
    THROW (DPST)

Figure C–1––Continued––(4 of 5).

NAME	SYMBOL

SWITCHES (CONTINUED)

KNIFE SWITCH, TRIPLE-POLE SINGLE-THROW (TPST)

KNIFE SWITCH, SINGLE-POLE DOUBLE-THROW (SPDT)

KNIFE SWITCH, DOUBLE-POLE DOUBLE-THROW (DPDT)

KNIFE SWITCH, TRIPLE-POLE DOUBLE-THROW (TPDT)

FIELD-DISCHARGE SWITCH WITH RESISTOR

PUSHBUTTON, NORMALLY OPEN (NO)

PUSHBUTTON NORMALLY CLOSED (NC)

PUSHBUTTON OPEN AND CLOSED (SPRING-RETURN)

NORMALLY CLOSED LIMIT SWITCH CONTACT

NORMALLY OPEN LIMIT SWITCH CONTACT

THERMAL ELEMENT

TRANSFORMERS

I PHASE TWO-WINDING TRANSFORMER

AUTOTRANSFORMER SINGLE-PHASE

Figure C-1—Continued—(5 of 5).

Section II. REPAIR SHOP DIAGRAMS

C-4. Introduction

Electrical circuit diagrams are essential to a repairman's work. Many electrical circuit diagrams use in a repair shop are connection diagrams and controller diagrams. These diagrams are a form of pictorial shorthand which uses symbols rather than pictures of electrical equipment to indicate how separate pieces of electrical equipment are connected in a circuit to perform useful electromechanical functions.

C-5. Types of Repair Shop Diagrams

a. Schematic Diagrams. A simple form of repair shop diagram is a schematic diagram like the ones shown in figures C-2, C-3, and C4. Such a diagram shows how the lead wires from the windings of a generator or motor are connected to the power line.

b. Block Diagram. Both the circular and flat (extended) types of diagrams indicate the number of poles and the connection of the lead wires

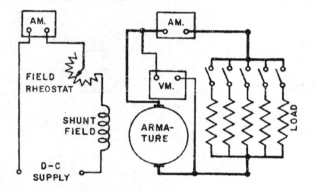

Figure C-2. Schematic wiring diagram of a separately excited generator.

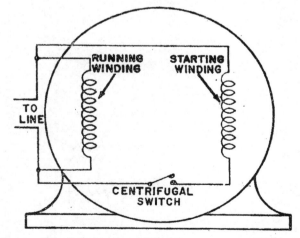

Figure C-3. Schematic wiring diagram of a split-phase motor.

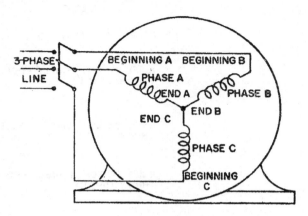

Figure C-4. Schematic wiring diagram of a star-connected, polyphase motor.

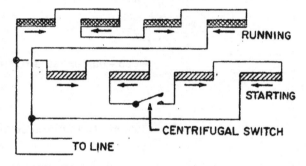

Figure C-5. Block diagram (extended type) of a four-pole, split-phase motor.

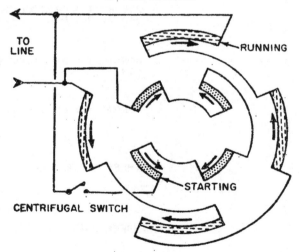

Figure C-6. Circular block diagram of a four-pole, split-phase motor.

from the windings to the power line (fig C-5, C-6, C-7, and C-8).

c. Connection Diagrams. The connection diagrams appearing in this manual should be used as a guide in developing an actual diagram of the unit under repair. At the time preliminary

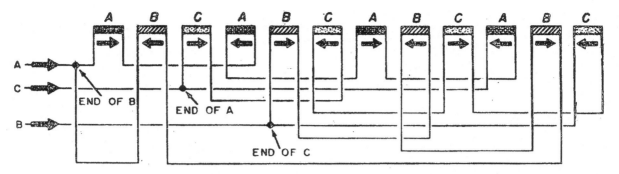

Figure C-7. Block diagram (extended type) of three-phase, four-pole, series-delta motor.

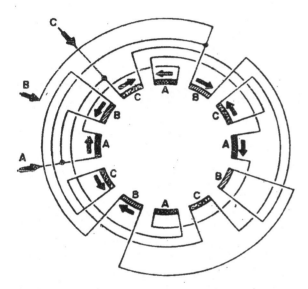

Figure C-8. Circular block diagram of a four-pole, three-phase, series-delta motor.

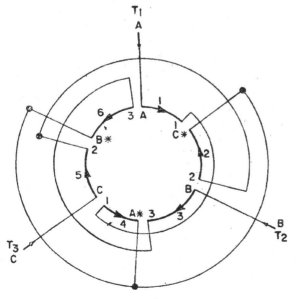

Figure C-9. Two-pole, three-phase, series-star connection.

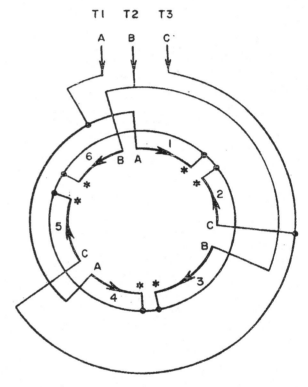

Figure C-10. Two-pole, three-phase, two-parallel-star connection.

data is taken, a diagram is developed for the particular unit under repair. For repair work, the block diagram is used to best advantage. Examples of connection diagrams are given in figures C-9 to C-21.

d. Controller Diagrams. Various types of controllers are used to run electrical machinery. The diagrams used to represent these controllers are elementary diagrams (fig C-22 to C-40) and complete wiring diagrams. Elementary diagrams reduce the concept of the operation to the simplest possible form by placing all parts necessary for the electromechanical operation of the

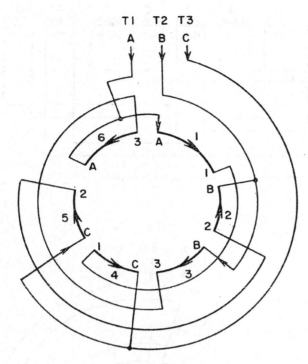

Figure C–11. Two-pole, three-phase, series-delta connection.

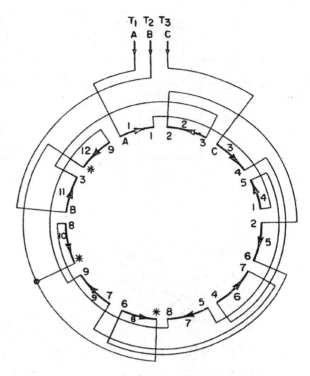

Figure C–13. Four-pole, three-phase, series-star connection.

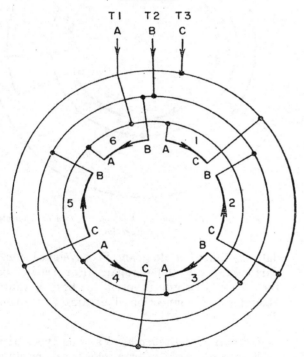

Figure C–12. Two-pole, three-phase, two-parallel-delta connection.

equipment in proximity to each other for clarity. In some elementary diagrams, however, where it is not possible to show all parts of the same equipment near to each other, code letters are used to designate the associated parts. For example, in figure C–24, coil M is used to operate main and auxiliary contractors M. Such a relationship between parts bearing the same designating letter must be remembered in studying elementary electrical circuit diagrams.

e. Wiring Diagram. Wiring diagrams indicate the actual relative position and connection of each wire, terminal, and component part of the electrical equipment. This type of diagram is illustrated in figures C–41, C–42, and C–43.

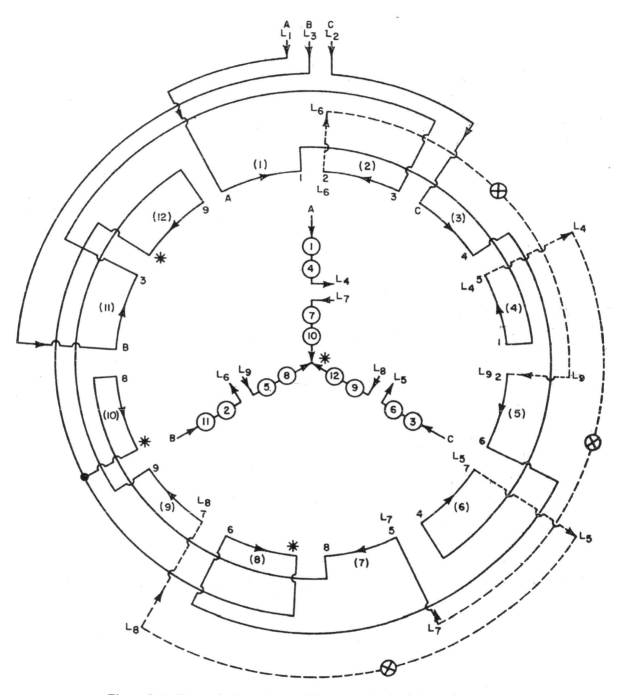

Figure C–14. Four-pole, three-phase, with three or nine leads for series-star or two-parallel-star connection.

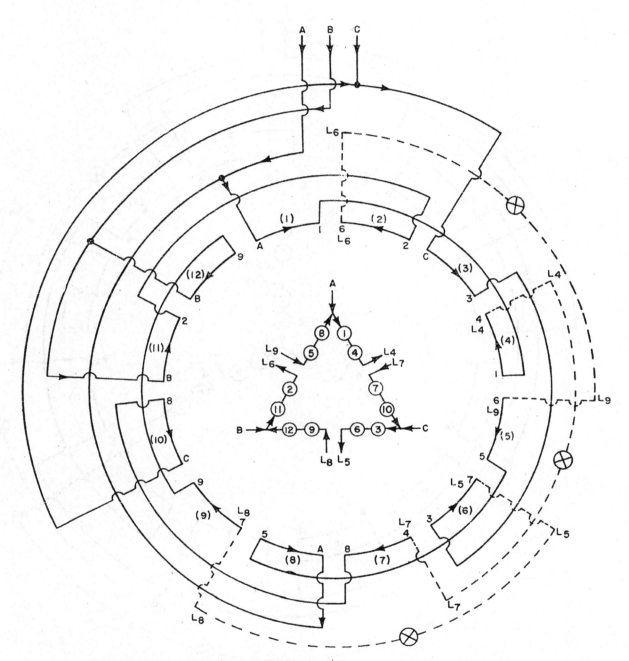

Figure C–15. Four-pole, three-phase, with three or nine leads for series-delta or two-parallel-delta connection.

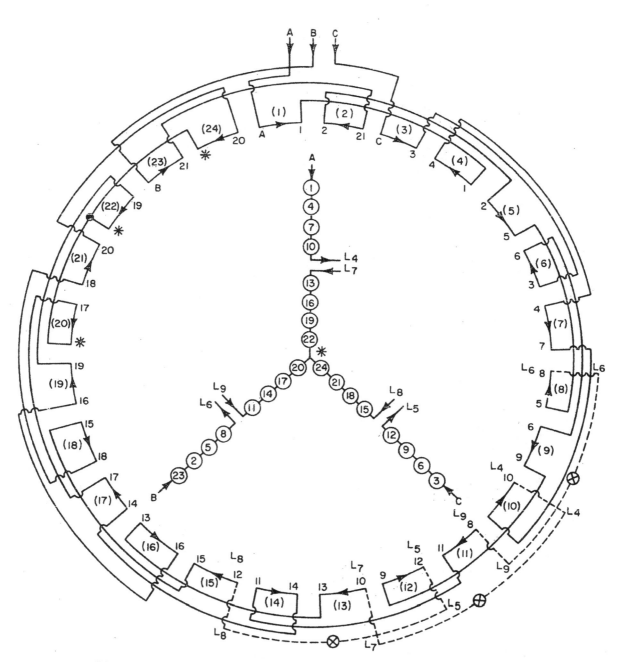

Figure C–16. Eight-pole, three-phase, with three or nine leads for series-star or parallel-star connection.

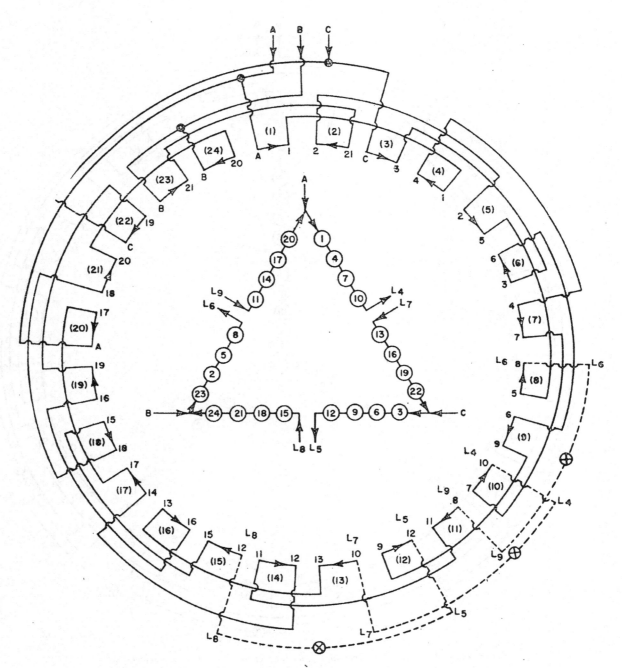

Figure C–17. Eight-pole, three-phase, with three or nine leads for series-delta or parallel-delta connection.

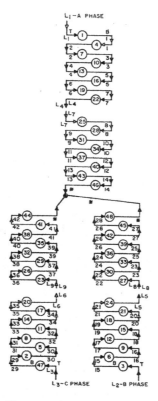

Figure C–18. Sixteen-pole, three-phase, nine-lead, series-star, or two-parallel-star connection.

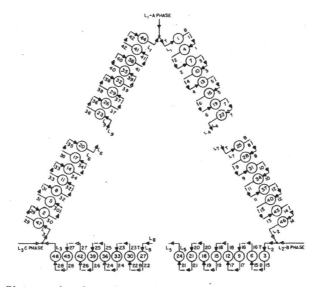

Figure C–19. Sixteen-pole, three-phase, nine-lead, series-delta, or two-parallel-delta connection.

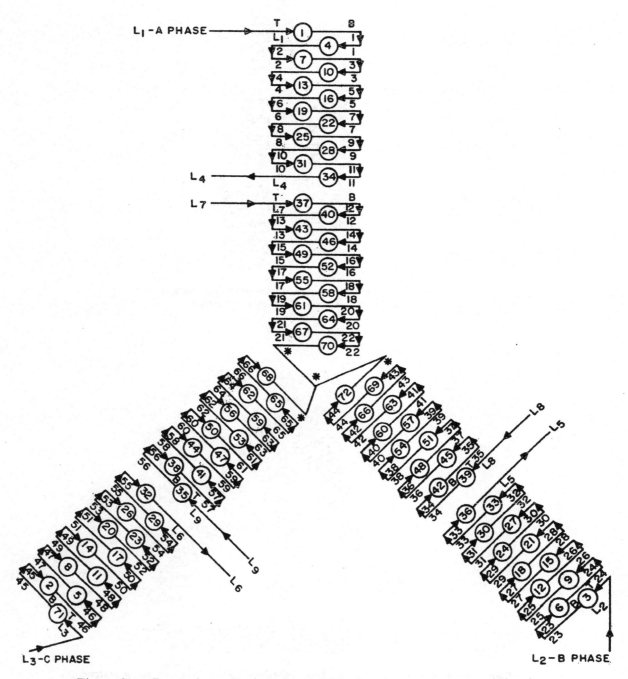

Figure C–20. Twenty-four-pole, three-phase, nine-lead, series-star, or two-parallel-star connection.

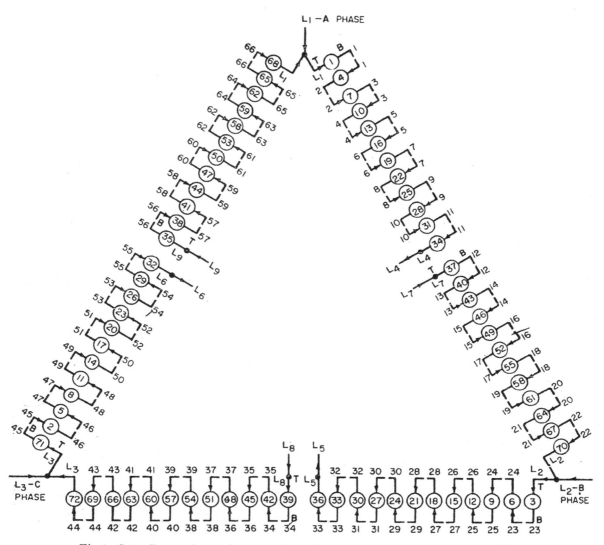

Figure C-21. Twenty-four-pole, three-phase, nine-lead, series-delta, or two-parallel-delta connection.

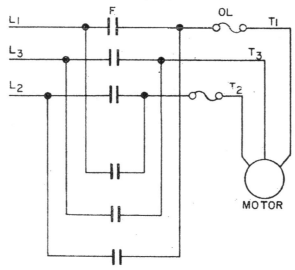

Figure C-22. An elementary motor-driven-power circuit diagram for an ac motor.

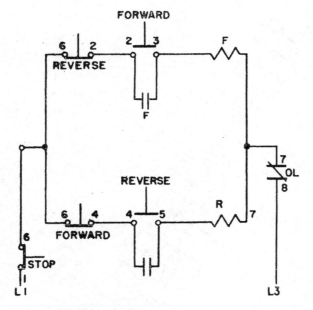

Figure C–23. An elementary motor-control circuit diagram
for an ac motor.

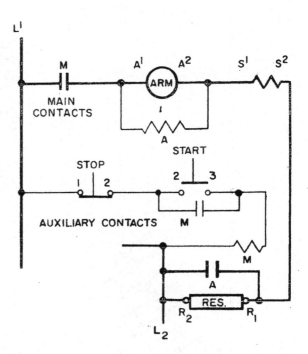

Figure C–24. An elementary control-and-power-circuit
diagram for a dc motor.

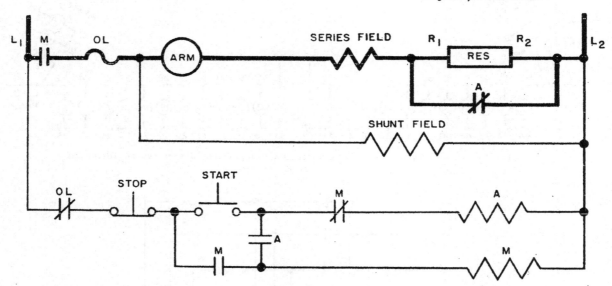

Figure C–25. An elementary schematic wiring diagram of a magnetic time-limit
controller.

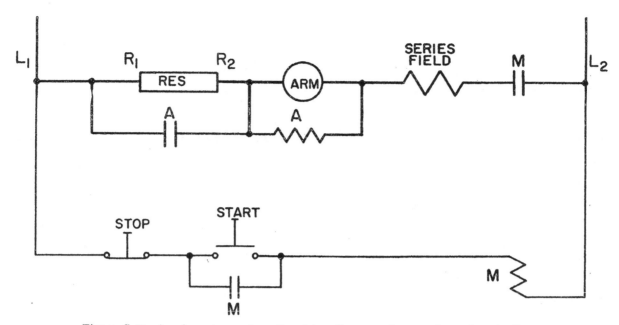

Figure C–26. An elementary schematic wiring diagram of a counter-emf controller.

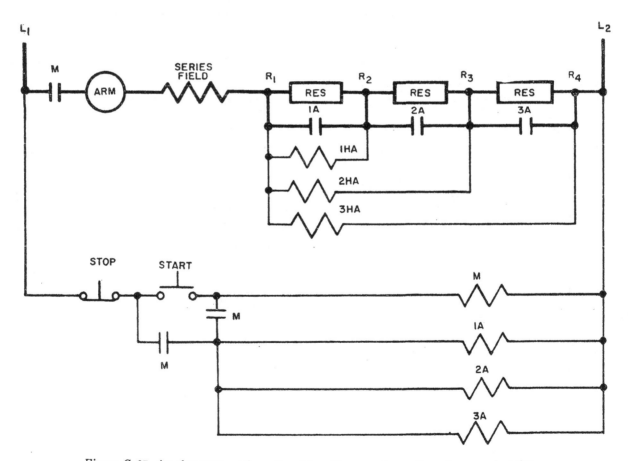

Figure C–27. An elementary schematic wiring diagram of a voltage-drop acceleration controller.

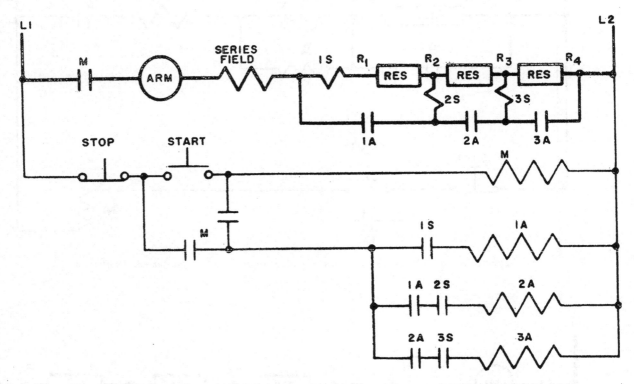

Figure C-28. An elementary schematic wiring diagram of a series-relay acceleration controller.

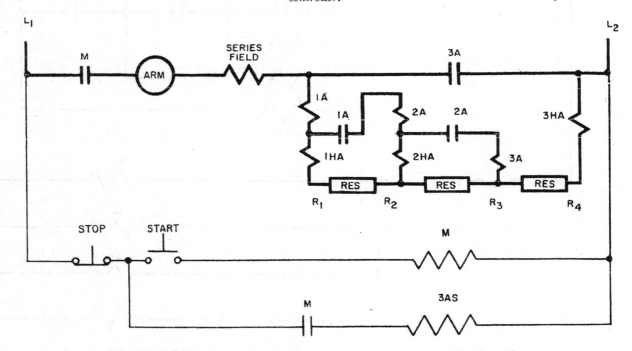

Figure C-29. An elementary schematic wiring diagram of a series-lockout-relay acceleration controller.

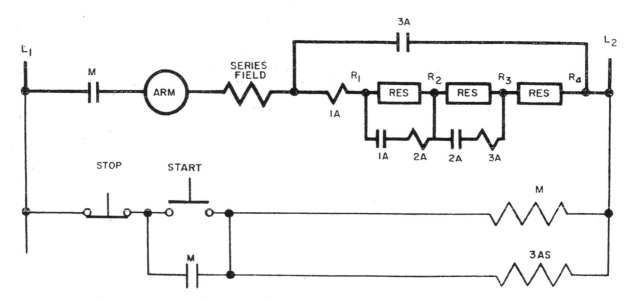

Figure C-30. An elementary schematic wiring diagram of a restricted iron-core lockout controller.

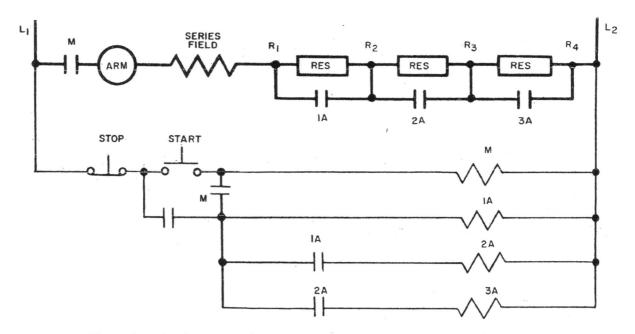

Figure C-31. An elementary schematic wiring diagram of an individual dashpot motor controller.

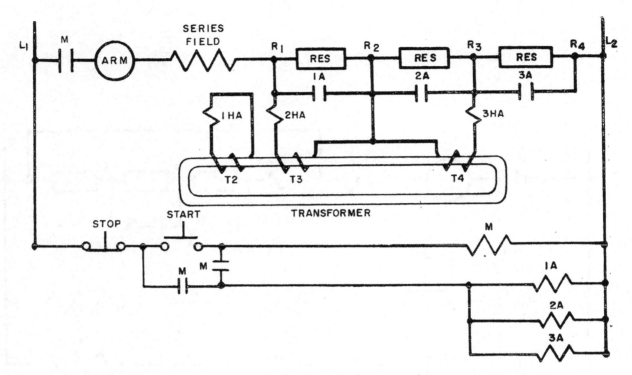

Figure C–32. An elementary schematic wiring diagram of an inductive time-limit controller.

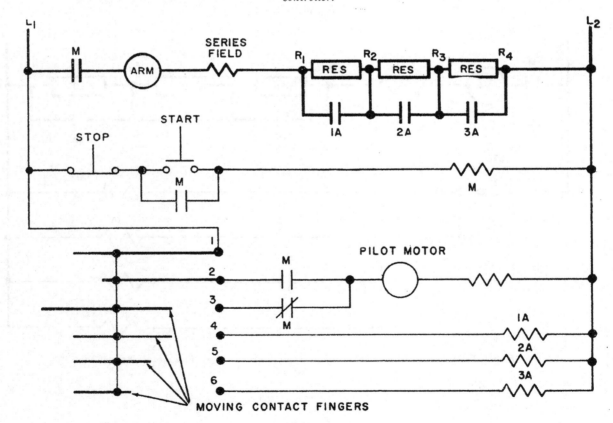

Figure C–33. An elementary schematic wiring diagram of a motor-driven time controller.

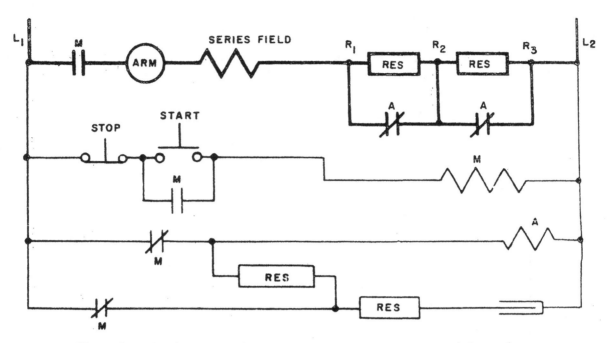

Figure C–34. An elementary schematic wiring diagram of a capacitor-timing starter.

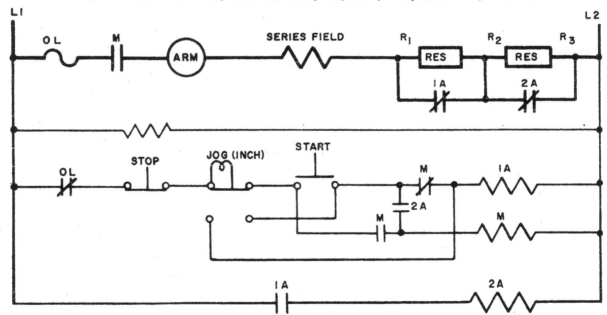

*Figure C–35. An elementary schematic wiring diagram of a magnetic time-delay
controller with jogging.*

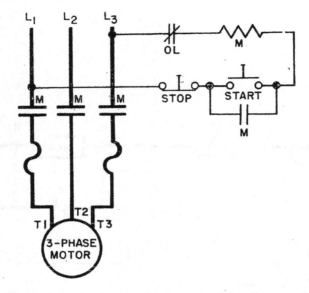

Figure C–36. An elementary schematic wiring diagram of
a magnetic, ac, across-the-line starter.

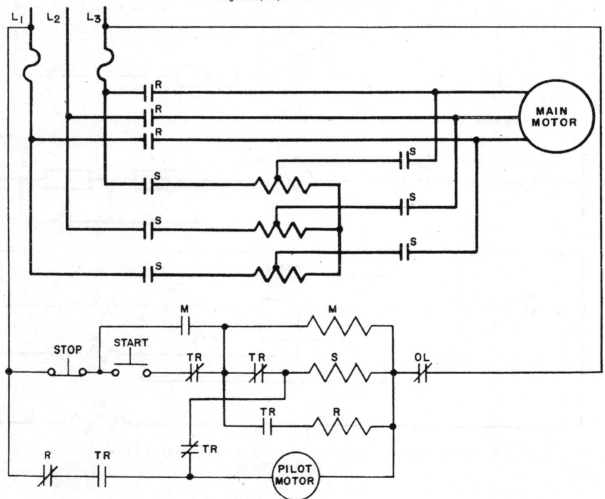

Figure C–37. An elementary schematic wiring diagram of a three-phase, compensator
type, automatic controller.

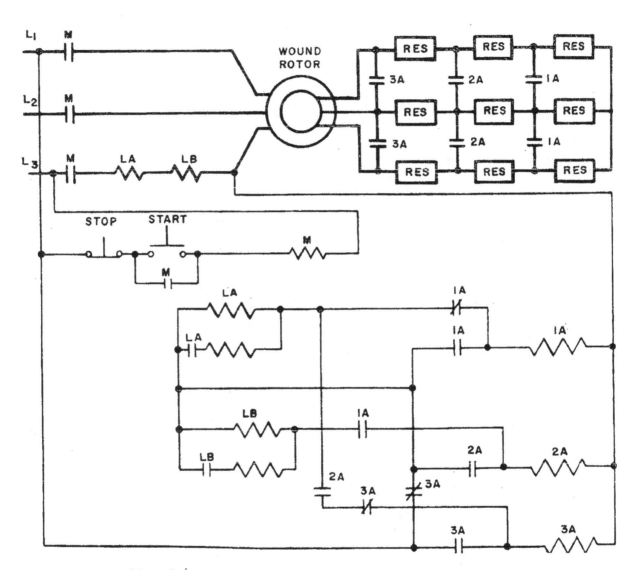

Figure C–38. An elementary schematic wiring diagram of a controller for a
wound-rotor motor.

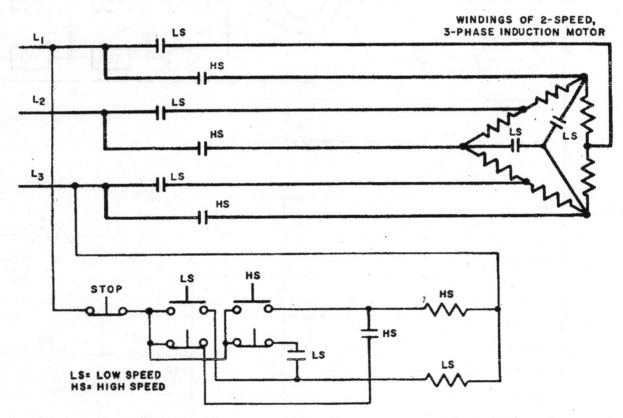

Figure C–39. An elementary schematic wiring diagram of an ac multispeed controller.

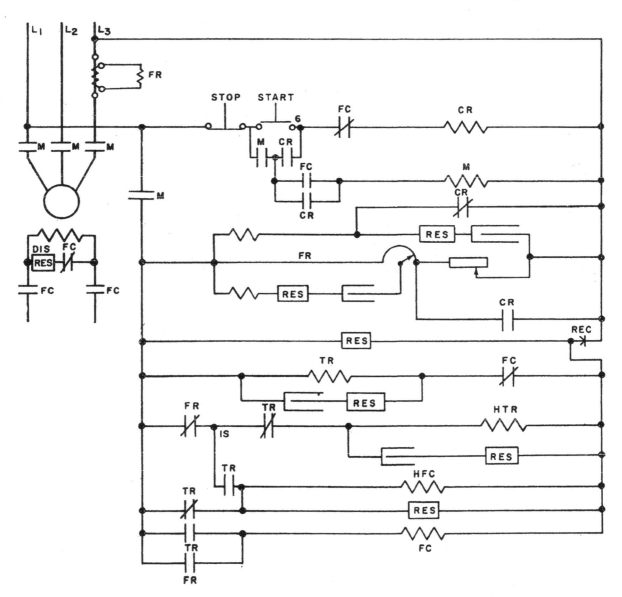

Figure C-40. An elementary schematic wiring diagram of a synchronous motor controller.

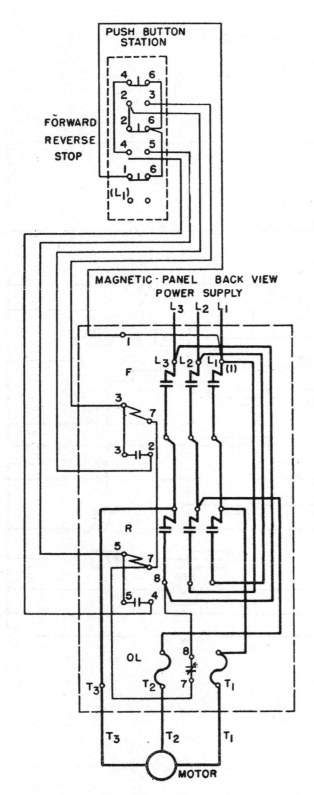

Figure C-41. A wiring diagram of a controller for an ac motor.

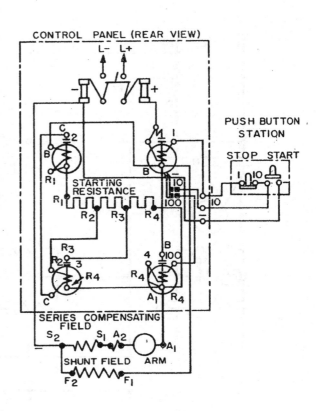

SCHEME OF MAIN CONNECTIONS

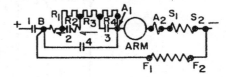

SEQUENCE OF SWITCHES

SW.	RUN			
1	o	o	o	o
2		o	o	
3			o	
4				o

Figure C-42. A wiring diagram of a controller with three starting steps for a dc motor.

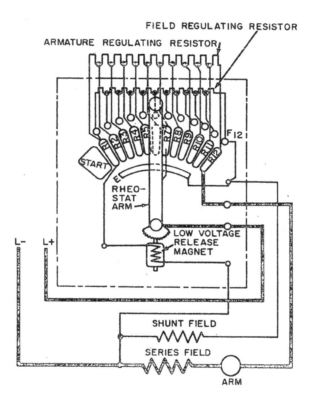

Figure C–43. A starting and speed-regulating rheostat
having both armature and field resistors.

GLOSSARY OF SEWAGE TREATMENT TERMS

CONTENTS

GLOSSARY OF SEWAGE TREATMENT TERMS

A

Activated Sludge Process.—See **Process, Activated Sludge.**

Acre-Foot.—A unit of volume used to express the amount of material in a trickling filter. A depth of one foot on an area of one acre is an acre-foot. Regardless of shape, 43,560 cubic feet is equivalent to one acre foot.

Adsorption.—The adherence of dissolved, colloidal, or finely divided solids on the surfaces of solid bodies with which they are brought into contact.

Aeration.—The bringing about of intimate contact between air and a liquid by one of the following methods: Spraying the liquid in the air; or by agitation of the liquid to promote surface absorption of air.

>**Diffused Air.**—Aeration produced in a liquid by air passed through a diffuser.

>**Mechanical.**— (1) The mixing, by mechanical means, of sewage and activated sludge, in the aeration tank of the activated sludge process, to bring fresh surfaces of liquid into contact with the atmosphere. (2) The introduction of atmospheric oxygen into a liquid by the mechanical action of paddle or spray mechanisms.

>**Modified.**—A modification of the activated sludge process in which a shortened period of aeration is employed with a reduced quantity of suspended solids in the mixed liquor.

>**Paddle-Wheel.**—The mechanical agitation of sewage in the aeration tanks of the activated sludge process by means of paddle wheels.

>**Spiral Flow.**—A method of diffusing air in an aeration tank of the activated sludge process, where, by means of properly designed baffles, and the proper location of diffusers, a spiral or helical movement is given to the air and the tank liquor.

>**Stage.**—Division of activated sludge treatment into stages with intermediate settling tanks and return of sludge in each stage.

>**Step.**—A procedure for adding increments of sewage along the line of flow in the aeration tanks of an activated sludge plant.

>**Tapered.**—The method of supplying varying amounts of air into the different parts of an aeration tank in the activated sludge process, more at the inlet, less near the outlet, and approximately proportional to the oxygen demand of the mixed liquor under aeration.

Algae.—Primitive plants, one or many-celled, usually aquatic and capable of elaborating their foodstuffs by photosynthesis.

Algicide.—Any substance which kills algae.

Alkaline.—Water or soils containing sufficient amounts of alkaline substances to raise the pH above 7.0, or to harm the growth of crops.

Alkalinity.—A term used to represent the content of carbonates, bicarbonates, hydroxides, and occasionally borates, silicates, and phosphates in water. It is expressed in parts per million of calcium carbonate.

Alum.—A common name for aluminum sulfate.

Arrester, Flame.—A safety device on a gas line which allows gas, but not a flame, to pass through.

B

Bacteria.—Primitive plants, generally free of pigment, which reproduce by dividing in one, two, or three planes. They occur as single cells, groups, chains, or filaments, and do not require light for their life processes. They may be grown by special culturing out of their native habitat.

Aerobic.—Bacteria which require free (elementary) oxygen for their growth.

Anaerobic.—Bacteria which grow in the absence of free oxygen and derive oxygen from breaking down complex substances.

Coli-Aerogenes.—See Bacteria, Coliform Group.

Coliform Group.—A group of bacteria, predominantly inhabitants of the intestine of man but also found on vegetation, including all aerobic and facultative anaerobic grain-negative, non-spore-forming bacilli that ferment lactose with gas formation. This group includes five tribes of which the very great majority are Eschericheae. The Eschericheae tribe comprises three genera and ten species, of which *Escherichia Coli* and *Aerobacter Aerogenes* are dominant. *The Escherichia Coli* are normal inhabitants of the intestine of man and all vertebrates whereas Aerobacter Aerogenes normally are found on grain and plants, and only to a varying degree in the intestine of man and animals. Formerly referred to as *B.Coli*, B.Coli group, *ColiAerogenes Group.*

Facultative Anaerobic.—Bacteria which can adapt themselves to growth in the presence, as well as in the absence, of uncombined oxygen.

Parasitic.—Bacteria which thrive on other living organisms.

Pathogenic.—Bacteria which can cause disease.

Saprophytic.—Bacteria which thrive upon dead organic matter.

Bacterial Count.—A measure of the concentration of bacteria.

Most Probable Number.—See Page 10.

Plate.—Number of colonies of bacteria grown on selected solid media at a given temperature and incubation period, usually expressed as the number of bacteria per milliliter of sample.

Bed, Sludge.—An area comprising natural or artificial layers of porous material upon which digested sewage sludge is dried by drainage and evaporation. A sludge bed may be opened to the atmosphere or covered usually with a greenhouse-type superstructure. Also called Sludge Drying Bed.

Biochemical.—Resulting from biologic growth or activity, and measured by or expressed in terms of the ensuing chemical change.

Biochemical Action.—Chemical changes resulting from the metabolism of living organisms.

Biochemical Oxygen Demand (BOD).—The quantity of oxygen utilized in the biochemical oxidation of organic matter in a specified time and at a specified temperature. It is not related to the oxygen requirements in chemical combustion, being determined entirely by the availability of the material as a biological food and by the amount of oxygen utilized by the microorganisms during oxidation.

Biochemical Oxygen Demand, Standard.—Biochemical oxygen demand as determined under standard laboratory procedure for five days at 20°C, usually expressed in parts per million.

Buffer.—The action of certain solutions in opposing a change of composition, especially of hydrogen-ion concentration.

Burner, Waste Gas.—A device in a sewage treatment plant for burning the waste gas from a sludge-digestion tank.

C

Centrifuge.—A mechanical device utilizing centrifugal force to separate solids from liquids or for separating liquid emulsions.

Chamber.—A general term applied to a space enclosed by walls or to a compartment, often prefixed by a descriptive word, such as "grit chamber," "screen chamber," "discharge chamber," or "flushing chamber," indicating its function.

Chloramines.—Compounds of organic amines or inorganic ammonia with chlorine.

Chloride of Lime.—Obsolete term; see Chlorinated Lime.

Chlorinated Lime.—A combination of slaked lime and chlorine gas (also termed Bleaching Powder, Chloride of Lime, Hypochlorite of Lime, etc.). When dissolved in water, it serves as a source of chlorine.

Chlorination.—The application of chlorine.

> **Break-Point.**—The application of chlorine to water, sewage or industrial wastes containing free ammonia to provide free residual chlorination.
>
> **Post.**—The application of chlorine to water, sewage, or industrial wastes subsequent to any treatment. The term refers only to a point of application.
>
> **Pre.**—The application of chlorine to water, sewage, or industrial wastes prior to any treatment. This term refers only to a point of application.

Chlorine.—An element, when uncombined, exists as a greenish yellow gas about 2.5 times as heavy as air. Under atmospheric pressure and at a temperature of —30.1°F the gas becomes an amber liquid about 1.5 times as heavy as water. The chemical symbol of chlorine is Cl, UP atomic weight is 35.457, and its molecular weight is 70.914.

> **Available.**—A term used in rating chlorinated lime and hypochlorites as to their total oxidizing power.
>
> **Combined Available Residual.**—That portion of the total residual chlorine remaining in water, sewage, or industrial wastes at the end of a specified contact period, which will react chemically and biologically as chloramines, or organic chloramines.
>
> **Demand.**—The difference between the amount of chlorine added to water, sewage, or industrial wastes and the amount of residual chlorine remaining at the end of a specified contact period. The demand for any given water varies with the amount of chlorine applied, time of contact, and temperas pure.
>
> **Dose.**—The amount of chlorine applied to a liquid, usually expressed in parts per million, or pounds per million gallons.
>
> **Free Available Residual.**—That portion of the total residual chlorine remaining in water. sewage, or industrial wastes at the end of a specified contact period. which will react chemically and biologically as hypochlorous acid, hypochlorite ion, or molecular chlorine.
>
> **Liquid.**—An article of commerce. Chlorine gas is generally manufactured by the electrolysis of a solution of common salt. The gas is dried and purified and is then liquefied by a combination of compression and refrigeration. Liquid chlorine is shipped under pressure in steel containers.
>
> **Residual.**--The total amount of chlorine (combined and free available chlorine) remaining in water, sewage, or industrial wastes at the end of a specified contact period following chlorination.
>
> **Test, Iodometric.**—The determination of residual chlorine in water, sewage, or industrial wastes by adding potassium iodide and titrating the liberated iodine with a standard solution of sodium thiosulfate, using starch solution as a colorimetric indicator.

Test, Ortho-Tolidine.—The determination of residual chlorine in water, sewage, or industrial wastes, using ortho-tolidine reagent and colorimetric standards.

Clarifier.—See Tank, Sedimentation.

Coagulation.—(1) The agglomeration of colloidal or finely divided suspended matter by the addition to the liquid of an appropriate chemical coagulant, by biological processes, or by other means. (2) The process of adding a coagulant and the necessary reacting chemicals.

Coils, Digester.—A system of pipes for hot water or steam installed in a sludge-digestion tank for the purpose of heating the sludge.

Coli-Aerogenes, or Coliform Group.—See Bacteria, Coliform Group.

Collector, Grit.—A device placed in a grit chamber to convey deposited grit to one end of the chamber for removal.

    Scum.—A mechanical device for skimming and removing scum from the surface of settling tanks.

    Sludge.—A mechanical device for scraping the sludge on the bottom of a settling tank to a sump, from which it can be drawn by hydrostatic or mechanical action.

Colloids.—Finely divided solids which will not settle but may be removed by coagulation or biochemical action.

Comminution.—The process of screening sewage and cutting the screenings into particles sufficiently fine to pass through the screen openings.

Concentration, Hydrogen-Ion.—See pH.

Copperas.—A common name for ferrous sulfate.

Copperas, Chlorinated.—A solution of ferrous sulfate and ferric chloride produced by chlorinating a solution of ferrous sulfate.

Cross Connection.—In plumbing, a physical connection through which a supply of potable water could be contaminated, polluted, or infected. A physical connection between water supplies from different systems.

Cubic Foot per Second.—A unit of discharge for measurement of flowing liquid, equal to a flow of one cubic foot per second past a given section. Also called Second-Foot.

D

Decomposition of Sewage.—The breakdown of the organic matter in sewage through aerobic and anaerobic processes.

Denitrification.—The reduction of nitrates in solution by biochemical action.

Deoxygenation.—The depletion of the dissolved oxygen in a liquid. Under natural conditions associated with the biochemical oxidation of organic matter present.

Detritus.—The sand, grit, and other coarse material removed by differential sedimentation in a relatively short period of detention.

Diffuser.—A porous plate or tube through which air is forced and divided into minute bubbles for diffusion in liquids. Commonly made of carborundum, alundum, or silica sand.

Digester.—A tank in which the solids resulting from the sedimentation of sewage are stored for the purpose of permitting anaerobic decomposition to the point of rendering the product nonputrescible and inoffensive. Erroneously termed digestor.

Digestion.—The processes occurring in a digester.

    Mesophilic.—Digestion by biological action at or below 113°F.

    Separate Sludge.—The digestion of sludge in separate tanks in which it is placed after it has been allowed to settle in other tanks.

Single-Stage Sludge.—Sludge digestion limited to a single tank for the entire digestion period.

Stage.—The digestion of sludge progressively in several tanks arranged in series.

Thermophilic.—Digestion carried on at a temperature generally between 113°F and 145°F.

Dilution. — (1) A method of disposing of sewage, industrial waste, or sewage treatment plant effluent by discharging it into a stream or body of water. (2) The ratio of volume of flow of a stream to the total volume of sewage or sewage treatment, ant effluent discharged into it.

Disinfection.—The killing of the larger portion (but not necessarily all) of the harmful and objectional microorganisms in, or on, a medium by means of chemicals, heat, ultraviolet light, etc.

Distributor.—A device used to apply liquid to the surface of a filter or contact bed, of two general types, fixed o movable. The fixed type may consist of perforated pipes or notched troughs, sloping boards, or sprinkler nozzles. The movable type may consist of rotating disks or rotating, reciprocating, or traveling perforated pipes or troughs applying a spray, or a thin sheet of liquid.

Dosing Tank.—A tank into which raw or partly treated sewage is introduced and held until the desired quantity has been accumulated, after which it is discharged at such a rate as may be necessary for the subsequent treatment.

Dryer.—A device utilizing heat to remove water.

Flash.—A device for vaporizing water from partly dewatered and finely divided sludge through contact with a current of hot gas or superheated vapor. Included is a squirrel cage mill for separating the sludge cake into fine particles.

Rotary.—A long steel cylinder, slowly revolving, with its long axis slightly inclined, through which passes the material to be dried in hot air. The material passes through from inlet to outlet, tumbling about.

E

E. Coli.—(Escherichia Coli).—A species of genus Escherichia bacteria, normal inhabitant of the intestine of man and all vertebrates. This species is classified among the Coliform Group. See Bacteria, Coliform Group.

Efficiency.—The ratio of the actual performance of a device to the theoretically perfect performance usually expressed as a percentage.

Average.—The efficiency of a machine or mechanical device over the range of load through which the machine operates.

Filter.—The operating results from a filter as measured by various criteria such as percentage reduction in suspended matter, total solids, biochemical oxygen demand, bacteria, color, etc.

Pump.—The ratio of energy converted into useful work to the energy applied to the pump shaft, or the energy difference in the water at the discharge and suction nozzles divided by the energy input at the pump shaft.

Wire-to-Water.—The ratio of the mechanical output of a pump, to the electrical input at the meter.

Effluent.—(1) A liquid which flows out of a containing space. (2) Sewage, water, or other liquid, partially or completely treated, or in its natural state, as the case may be, flowing out of a reservoir, basin, or treatment plant, or part thereof.

Final.—The effluent from the final unit of a sewage treatment plant.

Stable.—A treated sewage which contains enough oxygen to satisfy its oxygen demand.

6

Ejector, Pneumatic.—A device for raising sewage, sludge, or other liquid by alternately admitting such through an inward swinging check valve into the bottom of an airtight pot and then discharging it through an outward swinging check valve by admitting compressed air to the pot above the liquid.

Elutriation.—A process of sludge conditioning in which certain constituents are removed by successive decantations with fresh water or plant effluent, thereby reducing the demand for conditioning chemicals.

F

Factor.—Frequently a ratio used to express operating conditions.

Load.—The ratio of the average load carried by any operation to the maximum load carried, during a given period of time, expressed as a percentage. The load may consist of almost anything, such as electrical power, number of persons served, amount of water carried by a conduit, etc.

Power.—An electrical term describing the ratio of the true power passing through an electric circuit to the product of the volts times the amperes in the circuit. It is a measure of the lag or lead of the current in respect to the voltage. While the power of a current is the product of the voltage times the amperes in the circuit, in alternating current the voltage and amperes are not always in phase, hence the true power may be less than that determined by the product of volts times amperes.

Filter.—A term meaning (1) an oxidizing bed (2) a device for removing solids from a liquid by some type of strainer.

Biological.—A bed of sand, gravel, broken stone, or other media through which sewage flows or trickles, which depends on biological action for its effectiveness.

High-Rate.—A trickling filter operated at a high average daily dosing rate usually between 10-30 mgd per acre, sometimes including recirculation of effluent.

Low-Rate.—A trickling filter designed to receive a small load of BOD per unit volume of filtering material and to have a low dosage rate per unit of surface area (usually 1 to 4 mgd per acre). Also called Standard Rate Filter.

Roughing.—A sewage filter of relatively coarse material operated at a high rate as a preliminary treatment.

Sand.—A filter in which sand is used as a filtering medium.

Sand Sludge.—A bed of sand used to dewater sludge by drainage and evaporation.

Sludge.—The solid matter in sewage that is removed by settling in primary and secondary settling tanks.

Trickling.—A treatment unit consisting of a material such as broken stone, clinkers, slate, slats, or brush, over which sewage is distributed and applied in drops, films, or spray, from troughs, drippers, moving distributors, or fixed nozzles, and through which it trickles to the underdrains, giving opportunity for the formation of zoological slimes which clarify and oxidize the sewage.

Vacuum.—A filter consisting of a cylindrical drum mounted on a horizontal axis, covered with filtering material made of wool, felt, cotton, saran, nylon, dacron, polyethylene or similar substance, by stainless steel coil springs or metal screen, revolving with a partial submergence in the liquid. A vacuum is maintained under the cloth for the larger part of a revolution to extract moisture. The cake is scraped off continuously.

Filtrate.—The effluent of a Filter.

Floc.—Small gelatinous masses, formed in a liquid by the addition of coagulants thereto or through biochemical processes or by agglomeration.

Flocculator.—An apparatus for the formation of floc in water or sewage.

Flotation.—A method of raising suspended matter to the surface of the liquid in a tank as scum—by aeration, by the evolution of gas, chemicals, electrolysis, heat, or bacterial decomposition—and the subsequent removal of the scum by skimming.

Freeboard.—The vertical distance between the normal maximum level of the surface of the liquid in a conduit, reservoir, tank, canal, etc., and the top of the sides of an open conduit, the top of a dam or levee, etc., which is provided so that waves and other movements of the liquid will not overtop the confining structure.

Fungi.—Small nonchlorophyll-bearing plants which lack roots, stems, or leaves and which occur (among other places) in water, sewage, or sewage effluents, growing best in the absence of light. Their decomposition after death may cause disagreeable tastes and odors in water; in some sewage treatment processes they are helpful and in others they are detrimental.

G

Gage.—A device for measuring any physical magnitude.

    Float.—A device for measuring the elevation of the surface of a liquid, the actuation element being a buoyant float which rests upon the surface of the liquid.

    Indicator.—A gage that shows by means of an index, pointer, dial, etc., the instantaneous value of such characteristics as depth, pressure, velocity, stage, discharge, or the movements or positions of water-controlling devices.

    Mercury.—A gage wherein pressure of a fluid is measured by the height of a column of mercury which the fluid pressure will sustain. The mercury is usually contained in a tube, attached to the vessel or pipe containing the fluid.

    Pressure.—A device for registering the pressure of solids, liquids, or gases. It may be graduated to the register pressure in any units desired.

Garbage, Ground.—Garbage shredded or ground by apparatus installed in sinks and discharged to the sewerage system; or garbage collected and hauled to a central grinding station, shredded preliminary to disposal, usually, by digestion with sewage sludge.

Gas.—One of the three states of matter.

    Sewage.—(1) The gas produced by the septicization of sewage. (2) The gas produced during the digestion of sewage sludge, usually collected and utilized.

    Sewer.—Gas evolved in sewers from the decomposition of the organic matter in the sewage. Also any gas present in the sewerage system, even though it is from gas mains, gasoline, cleaning fluid, etc.

Gasification.—The transformation of sewage solids into gas in the decomposition of sewage.

Go Devil.—A scraper with self-adjusting spring blades, inserted in a pipe line, and carried forward by the fluid pressure for clearing away accumulations, tuberculations, etc.

Grade.—(1) The inclination or slope of a stream channel, conduit, or natural ground surface, usually expressed in terms of the ratio or percentage of number of units of vertical rise or fall per unit of horizontal distance. (2) The elevation of the invert of the bottom of a pipe line, canal, culvert, sewer, etc. (3) The finished surface of a canal bed, road bed, top of an embankment. or bottom of an excavation. (4) In plumbing, the fall in inches per foot of length of pipe.

Grease.—In sewage, grease including fats, waxes, free fatty acids, calcium and magnesium soaps, mineral oils, and other non-fatty materials. The type of solvent used for its extraction should be stated.

Grinder, Screenings.—A device for grinding, shredding, or comminuting material removed from sewage by screens.

Grit.—The heavy mineral matter in water or sewage, such as gravel, cinders, etc.

H

Head.—Energy per unit weight of liquid at a specified point. It is expressed in feet.

    Dynamic.—The head against which a pump works.

    Friction.—The head lost by water flowing in a stream or conduit as the result of the disturbances set up by the contact between the moving water and its containing conduit, and by intermolecular friction. In laminar flow the head lost is approximately proportional to the first power of the velocity; in turbulent flow to a higher power, approximately the square of the velocity. While strictly speaking, head losses due to bends, expansions, obstructions, impact, etc., are not included in this term, the usual practice is to include all such head losses under this term.

    Loss of.—The decrease in head between two points.

    Static.—The vertical distance between the free level of the source of supply, and the point of free discharge, or the level of the free surface.

    Total Dynamic.—The difference between the elevation corresponding to the pressure at the discharge flange of a pump and the elevation corresponding to the vacuum or pressure at the suction flange of the pump, corrected to the same datum plane, plus the velocity head at the discharge flange of the pump, minus the velocity head at the suction flange of the pump. It includes the friction head.

    Velocity.—The theoretical vertical height through which a liquid body may be raised due to its kinetic energy. It is equal to the square of the velocity divided by twice the acceleration due to gravity.

Humus.—The dark or black carboniferous residue in the soil resulting from the decomposition of vegetable tissues of plants originally growing therein. Residues similar in appearance and behavior are found in well-digested sludges and in activated sludge.

Hypochlorite.—Compounds of chlorine in which the radical (OC1) is present. They are usually inorganic.

    High Test.—A solid triple salt containing Ca (OC1) 2 to the extent that the fresh solid has approximately 70 percent available chlorine. It is not the same as chlorinated lime.

    Sodium.—A solution containing NaOC1, prepared by passing chlorine into solutions of soda ash, or reacting soda ash solutions with high-test hypochlorites and decanting from the precipitated sludge.

I

Imhoff Cone.—A conically shaped graduated glass vessel used to measure approximately the volume of settleable solids in various liquids of sewage origin.

Imhoff Tank.—See Tank, Imhoff

Impeller.—The rotating part of a centrifugal pump, containing the curved vanes.

    Closed.—An impeller having the side walls extended from the outer circumference of the suction opening to the vane tips.

    Nonclogging.—An impeller of the open, closed, or semi-closed type designed with large passages for passing large solids.

Open.—An impeller without attached side walls.

Screw.—The helical impeller of a screw pump.

Index, Sludge Volume.—The volume is milliliters occupied by one gram of dry solids after the aerated mixed liquor settles 30 minutes, commonly referred to as the Mohlman index.

Influent.—Sewage, water, or other liquid, raw or partly treated, flowing into a reservoir, basin, or treatment plant, or part thereof.

L

Lagoon, Sludge.—A relatively shallow basin, or natural depression, used for the storage or digestion of sludge, and sometimes for its ultimate detention or dewatering.

Lift, Air.—A device for raising liquid by injecting air in and near the bottom of a riser pipe submerged in the liquid to be raised.

Liquefaction.—The changing of the organic matter in sewage from an insoluble to a soluble state, and effecting a reduction in its solid contents.

Liquor.—Any liquid.

Mixed.—A mixture of activated sludge and sewage in the aeration tank undergoing activated sludge treatment.

Supernatant. — (1) The liquor overlying deposited solids. (2) The liquid in a sludge-digestion tank which lies between the sludge at the bottom and the floating scum at the top.

Loading.—The time rate at which material is applied to a treatment device involving length, area, or volume or other design factor.

BOD, Filter.—The pounds of oxygen demand in the applied liquid per unit of filter bed area, or volume of stone per day.

Weir.—Gallons overflow per day per foot of weir length.

M

Main, Force.—A pipe line on the discharge side of a water or sewage pumping station, usually under pressure.

Manometer.—An instrument for measuring pressure; usually it consists of a U-shaped tube containing a liquid, the surface of which in one end of the tube moves proportionally with changes in pressure upon the liquid in the other end. The term is also applied to a tube type of differential pressure gage.

Matter.—Solids, liquids, and gases.

Inorganic.—Chemical substances of mineral origin. They are not usually volatile with heat.

Organic.—Chemical substances of animal, vegetable and industrial origin. They include most carbon compounds, combustible and volatile with heat.

Suspended.—(1) Solids in suspension in sewage or effluent. (2) Commonly used for solids in suspension in sewage or effluent which can readily be removed by filtering in a laboratory.

Microorganism.—Minute organisms either plant or animal, invisible or barely visible to the naked eye.

Moisture, Percentage.—The water content of sludge expressed as the ratio of the loss in weight after drying at 103°C, to the original weight of the sample, multiplied by one hundred.

Mold.—See Fungi.

Most Probable Number, (MPN).—In the testing of bacterial density by the dilution method, that number of organisms per unit volume which, in accordance with statistical theory, would be more likely than any other possible number to yield the observed test result or which would yield the observed test result with the greatest frequency. Expressed as density of organisms per 100 ml.

N

Nitrification.—The oxidation of ammonia nitrogen into nitrates through biochemical action.

O

Overflow Rate.—One of the criteria for the design of settling tanks in treatment plants; expressed in gallons per day per square foot of surface area in the settling tank. See Surface Settling Rate.

Oxidation.—The addition of oxygen, removal of hydrogen, or the increase in the valence of an element.

　Biochemical.—See Oxidation, Sewage.

　Biological.—See Oxidation, Sewage.

　Direct.—Oxidation of substances in sewage without the benefit of living organisms, by the direct application of air or oxidizing agents such as chlorine.

　Sewage.—The process whereby, through the agency of living organisms in the presence of oxygen, the organic matter contained in sewage is converted into a more stable form.

Oxygen.—A chemical element.

　Available.—The quantity of uncombined or free oxygen dissolved in the water of a stream.

　Balance.—The relation between the biochemical oxygen demand of a sewage or treatment plant effluent and the oxygen available in the diluting water.

　Consumed.—The quantity of oxygen taken from potassium permanganate in solution by a liquid containing organic matter. Commonly regarded as an index of the carbonaceous matter present. Time and temperature must be specified. The chemical oxygen demand (COD) uses potassium dichromate.

　Deficiency.—The additional quantity of oxygen required to satisfy the biochemical oxygen demand in a given liquid. Usually expressed in parts per million.

　Dissolved.—Usually designated as DO. The oxygen dissolved in sewage, water or other liquid usually expressed in parts per million or percent of saturation.

　Residual.—The dissolved oxygen content of a stream after deoxygenation has begun.

　Sag.—A curve that represents the profile of dissolved oxygen content along the course of a stream, resulting from deoxygenation associated with biochemical oxidation of organic matter, and reoxygenation through the absorption of atmospheric oxygen and through biological photosynthesis.

P

Parts Per Million.—Milligrams per liter expressing the concentration of a specified component in a dilute sewage. A ratio of pounds per million pounds, grams per million grams, etc.

Percolation.—The flow or trickling of a liquid downward through a contact or filtering medium. The liquid may or may not fill the pores of the medium.

Period.—A time interval.

Aeration.—(1) The theoretical time, usually expressed in hours that the mixed liquor is subjected to aeration in an aeration tank undergoing activated sludge treatment; is equal to (a) the volume of the tank divided by (b) the volumetric rate of flow of the sewage and return sludge. (2) The theoretical time that water is subjected to aeration.

Detention.—The theoretical time required to displace the contents of a tank or unit at a given rate of discharge (volume divided by rate of discharge).

Flowing-Through.—The average time required for a small unit volume of liquid to pass through a basin from inlet to outlet. In a tank where there is no short-circuiting, and no spaces, the detention period and the flowing-through period are the same.

pH.—The logarithm of the reciprocal of the hydrogen-ion concentration. It is not the same as the alkalinity and cannot be calculated therefrom.

Plankton.—Drifting organisms, usually microscopic.

Pollution.—The addition of sewage, industrial wastes, or other harmful or objectionable material to water.

Ponding, Filter.—See Pooling, Filter.

Pooling, Filter.—The formation of pools of sewage on the surface of filters caused by clogging.

Population Equivalent.—(1) The calculated population which would normally contribute the same amount of biochemical oxygen demand (BOD) per day. A common base is 0.167 lb. of 5-day BOD per capita per day. (2) For an industrial waste, the estimated number of people contributing sewage equal in strength to a unit volume of the waste or to some other unit involved in producing or manufacturing a particular commodity.

Pre-Aeration.—A preparatory treatment of sewage comprising aeration to remove gases, add oxygen, or promote flotation of grease, and aid coagulation.

Precipitation, Chemical.—Precipitation induced by addition of chemicals.

Pressure.—Pounds per square inch or square foot.

    Atmospheric.—The pressure exerted by the atmosphere at any point. Such pressure decreases the elevation of the point above sea level increases. One atmosphere is equal to 14.7 lb. per sq. in., 29.92 in. or 760 mm of mercury column or 33.90 ft. of water column at average sea level under standard conditions.

    Hydrostatic.—The pressure, expressed as a total force per unit of area, exerted by a body of water at rest.

    Negative.—A pressure less than the local atmospheric pressure at a given point.

Process.—A sequence of operations.

    Activated Sludge.—A biological sewage treatment process in which a mixture of sewage and activated sludge is agitated and aerated. The activated sludge is subsequently separated from the treated sewage (mixed liquor) by sedimentation, and wasted or returned to the process as needed. The treated sewage overflows the weir of the settling tank in which separation from the sludge takes place.

    Biological.—The process by which the life activities of bacteria, and other microorganisms in the search for food, break down complex organic materials into simple, more stable substances. Self-purification of sewage-polluted streams, sludge digestion, and all so-called secondary sewage treatments result from this process. Also called Biochemical Process.

Pump.—A device used to increase the head on a liquid.

    Booster.—A pump installed on a pipe line to raise the pressure of the water on the discharge side of the pump.

Centrifugal, Fluid.—A pump consisting of an impeller fixed on a rotating shaft and enclosed in a casing, having an inlet and a discharge connection. The rotating impeller creates pressure in the liquid by the velocity derived from centrifugal force.

Centrifugal, Screw.—A centrifugal pump having a screw-type impeller; may be axial-flow, or combined axial and radial-flow, type.

Centrifugal, Closed.—A centrifugal pump where the impeller is built with the vanes enclosed within circular disks.

Diaphragm.—A pump in which a flexible diaphragm, generally of rubber, is the operating part; it is fastened at the outer rim; when the diaphragm is moved in one direction, suction is exerted and when it is moved in the opposite direction, the liquid is forced through a discharge valve.

Double-Suction.—A centrifugal pump with suction pipes connected to the casing from both sides.

Duplex.—A reciprocating pump consisting of two cylinders placed side by side and connected to the same suction and discharge pipe, the pistons moving so that one exerts suction while the other exerts pressure, with the result that the discharge from the pump is continuous.

Horizontal Screw.—A pump with a horizontal cylindrical casing, in which operates a runner with radial blades, like those of a ship's propeller. The pump has a high efficiency at low heads and high discharges, and is used extensively in drainage work.

Mixed Flow.—A centrifugal pump in which the head is developed partly by centrifugal force and partly by the lift of the vanes on the liquid.

Open Centrifugal.—A centrifugal pump where the impeller is built with a set of independent vanes.

Propeller.—A centrifugal pump which develops most of its head by the propelling or lifting action of the vanes on the liquids.

Purification.—The removal, by natural or artificial methods, or objectionable matter from water.

Putrefaction.—Biological decomposition of organic matter with the production of ill-smelling products associated with anaerobic conditions.

Putrescibility. — (1) The relative tendency of organic matter to undergo decomposition in the absence of oxygen. (2) The susceptibility of waste waters, sewage, effluent, or sludge to putrefaction. (3) Term used in water or sewage analysis to define stability of a polluted water or raw or partially treated sewage.

Q

Quicklime.—A calcined material, the major part of which is calcium oxide or calcium oxide in natural association with a lesser amount of magnesium oxide, capable of slaking with water.

R

Rack.—An arrangement of parallel bars.

Bar.—A screen composed of parallel bars, either vertical or inclined, placed in a waterway to catch floating debris, and from which the screenings may be raked. Also called rack.

Coarse.—A rack with 3/4 inch to 6 inch spaces between bars.

Fine.—Generally used for a screen or rack which has openings of 3/32 to 3/16 inches. Some screens have less than 3/32 inch openings.

Radius, Hydraulic.—The cross-sectional area of a stream of water divided by the length of that part of its periphery in contact with its containing conduit; the ratio of area to wetted perimeter.

Rate.—The result of dividing one concrete number by another.

Filtration.—The rate of application of water or sewage to a filter, usually expressed in million gallons per acre per day, or gallons per minute per square foot.

Infiltration.—The rate, usually expressed in cubic feet per second, or million gallons per day per mile of waterway, at which ground water enters an infiltration ditch or gallery, drain, sewer, or other underground conduit.

Surface Settling.—Gallons per day per square foot of free horizontal water surface. Used in design of sedimentation tanks.

Reaeration.—The absorption of oxygen by a liquid, the dissolved oxygen content of which has been depleted.

Reaeration, Sludge.—The continuous aeration of sludge after its initial aeration in the activated sludge process.

Recirculation. — (1) The refiltration of all or a portion of the effluent in a high-rate trickling filter for the purpose of maintaining a uniform high rate through the filter. (2) The return of effluent to the incoming flow to reduce its strength.

Reduction.—The decrease in a specific variable.

Over-All.—The percentage reduction in the final effluent as compared to the raw sewage.

Percentage.—The ratio of material removed from water or sewage by treatment, to the material originally present (expressed as a percentage).

Sludge.—The reduction in the quantity and change in character of sewage sludge as the result of digestion.

Regulator.—A device or apparatus for controlling the quantity of sewage admitted to an intercepting sewer or a unit of a sewage treatment plant.

Reoxygenation.—The replenishment of oxygen in a stream from (1) dilution water entering stream, (2) biological reoxygenation through the activities of certain oxygen-producing plants, and (3) atmospheric reaction.

Residual, Chlorine.—See Chlorine, residual.

Rotor.—The member of an electric generator or water wheel which rotates.

S

Screen.—A device with openings, generally of uniform size, used to retain or remove suspended or floating solids in flowing water or sewage, and to prevent them from entering an intake or passing a given point in a conduit. The screening element may consist of parallel bars, rods, wires, grating, wire mesh, or perforated plate, and the openings may be of any shape, although they are generally circular or rectangular. The device may also be used to segregate granular material, such as sand, crushed rock, and soil, into various sizes.

Scum.—A mass of sewage matter which floats on the surface of sewage.

Second-Foot.—An abbreviated expression for cubic foot per second.

Sedimentation.—The process of subsidence and deposition of suspended matter carried by water, sewage, or other liquids, by gravity. It is usually accomplished by reducing the velocity of the liquid below the point where it can transport the suspended material. Also called Settling. See Precipitation, Chemical.

Final.—Settling of partly settled, flocculated or oxidized sewage in a final tank.

Plain.—The sedimentation of suspended matter in a liquid unaided by chemicals or other special means, and without provision for the decomposition of deposited solids in contact with the sewage.

Seeding, Sludge.—The inoculation of undigested sewage solids with sludge that has undergone decomposition, for the purpose of introducing favorable organisms, thereby accelerating the initial stages of digestion.

Self-Purification.—The natural processes of purification in a moving or still body of water whereby the bacterial content is reduced, the BOD is largely satisfied, the organic content is stabilized, and the dissolved oxygen returned to normal.

Sewage.—Largely the water supply of a community after it has been fouled by various uses. From the standpoint of source it may be a combination of the liquid or water-carried wastes from residences, business buildings, and institutions, together with those from industrial establishments, and with such ground water, surface water, and storm water as may be present.

    Domestic.—Sewage derived principally from dwellings, business buildings, institutions, and the like. (It may or may not contain ground water, surface water, or storm water.)

    Fresh.—Sewage of recent origin containing dissolved oxygen at the point of examination.

    Industrial.—Sewage in which industrial wastes predominate.

    Stable.—Sewage in which the organic matter has been stabilized.

    Raw.—Sewage prior to receiving any treatment.

    Sanitary.—(1) Domestic sewage with storm and surface water excluded. (2) Sewage discharging from the sanitary conveniences of dwellings (including apartment houses and hotels), office buildings, factories, or institutions. (3) The water supply of a community after it has been used and discharged into a sewer.

    Septic.—Sewage undergoing putrefaction under anaerobic conditions.

    Settled.—Sewage from which most of the settleable solids have been removed by sedimentation.

    Stale.—A sewage containing little or no oxygen, but as yet free from putrefaction.

Sewer.—A pipe or conduit. generally closed, but normally not flowing full, for carrying sewage and other waste liquids.

    Branch.—A sewer which receives sewage from a relatively small area, and discharges into a main sewer.

    Combined.—A sewer receiving both surface runoff and sewage.

    House.—A pipe conveying sewage from a single building to a common sewer or point of immediate disposal.

    Intercepting.—A sewer which receives dry-weather flow from a number of transverse sewers or outlets and frequently additional predetermined quantities of storm water (if from a combined system), and conducts such waters to a point for treatment or disposal.

    Lateral.—A sewer which discharges into a branch or other sewer and has no other common sewer tributary to it.

    Main. — (1) A sewer to which one or more branch sewers are tributary. Also called Trunk Sewer. (2) In plumbing, the public sewer in a street, alley, or other premises under the jurisdiction of a municipality.

    Sanitary.—A sewer which carries sewage and to which storm, surface, and ground waters are not intentionally admitted.

    Separate.—See Sewer, Sanitary.

    Storm.—A sewer which carries storm water and surface water, street wash and other wash waters, or drainage, but excludes sewage and industrial wastes. Also called Storm Drain.

    Trunk—A sewer which receives many tributary branches and serves a large territory. See Sewer, Main.

    Outfall.—A sewer which receives the sewage from a collecting system and carries it to a point of final discharge.

Outlet.—The point of final discharge of sewage or treatment plant effluent.

Sewerage.—A comprehensive term which includes facilities for collecting, pumping, treating, and disposing of sewage; the sewerage system and the sewage treatment works.

Shredder.—A device for size reduction.

Screenings.—A device which disintegrates screenings.

Sludge.—An apparatus to break down lumps in air-dried digested sludge.

Siphon.—A closed conduit, a portion of which lies above the hydraulic grade line. This results in a pressure less than atmospheric in that portion, and hence requires that a vacuum be created to start flow.

Skimmer, Grease.—A device for removing floating grease or scum from the surface of sewage in a tank.

Skimming.—The process of removing floating grease or scum from the surface of sewage in a tank.

Sleek.—The thin oily film usually present which gives characteristic appearance to the surface of water into which sewage or oily waste has discharged. Also termed slick.

Sloughing.—The phenomenon associated with trickling filters and contact aerators. whereby slime and solids accumulated in the media are discharged with the effluent.

Sludge.—The accumulated settled solids deposited from sewage or industrial wastes, raw or treated. in tanks or basins, and containing more or less water to form a semiliquid mass.

Activated.—Sludge floc produced in raw or settled sewage by the growth of zoogleal bacteria and other organisms in the presence of dissolved oxygen, and accumulated in sufficient concentration by returning floc previously formed.

Bulking.—A phenomenon that occurs in activated sludge plants whereby the sludge occupies excessive volumes and will not concentrate readily.

Conditioning.—Treatment of liquid sludge preliminary to dewatering and drainability, usually by the addition of chemicals.

Dewatering.—The process of removing a part of the water in sludge by any method, such as draining, evaporation, pressing, centrifuging, exhausting, passing between rollers, or acid flotation, with or without heat. It involves reducing from a liquid to a spadable condition rather than merely changing the density of the liquid (concentration) on the one hand or drying (as in a kiln) on the other.

Digestion.—The process by which organic or volatile matter in sludge is gasified, liquefied, mineralized. or converted into more stable organic matter, through the activities of living organisms.

Humus.—See **Humus.**

Solids.—Material in the solid state.

Dissolved.—Solids which are present in solution.

Nonsettleable.—Finely divided suspended solids which will not subside in quiescent water, sewage, or other liquid in a reasonable period. Such period is commonly, though arbitrarily, taken as two hours.

Settleable.—Suspended solids which will subside in quiescent water, sewage, or other liquid in a reasonable period. Such period is commonly, though arbitrarily, taken as one hour. Also called Settling Solids.

Suspended.—The quantity of material deposited when a quantity of water, sewage, or other liquid is filtered through an asbestos mat in a Gooch crucible.

Total.—The solids in water, sewage, or other liquids; it includes the suspended solids (largely removable by filter paper) and the filterable solids (those which pass through filter paper).

16

Volatile.—The quantity of solids in water, sewage, or other liquid, lost on ignition of the total solids.

Squeegee.—(1) A device, generally with a soft rubber edge, used for dislodging and removing deposited sewage solids from the walls and bottoms of sedimentation tanks. (2) The metal blades attached to the lower arms of a clarifier mechanism to move the sludge along the tank bottom.

Stability.—The ability of any substance, such as sewage, effluent, or digested sludge, to resist putrefaction. It is the antonym of putrescibility.

Standard Methods.—Methods of analysis of water, sewage, and sludge approved by a Joint Committee of the American Public Health Association. American Water Works Association, and Federation of Sewage Works Associations.

Stator.—The stationary member of an electric generator or motor.

Sterilization.—The destruction of all living organisms, ordinarily through the agency of heat or of some chemical.

T

Tank.—A circular or rectangular vessel.

Detritus.—A detention chamber larger than a grit chamber, usually with provision for removing the sediment without interrupting the flow of sewage. A settling tank of short detention period designed, primarily, to remove heavy settleable solids.

Final Settling.—A tank through which the effluent from a trickling filter, or aeration or contact aeration tank flows for the purpose of removing the settleable solids.

Flocculating.—A tank used for the formation of floc by the agitation of liquids.

Imhoff.—A deep two-storied sewage tank originally patented by Karl Imhoff. consisting of an upper or continuous flow sedimentation chamber and a lower or sludge-digestion chamber. The floor of the upper chamber slopes steeply to trapped slots, through which solids may slide into the lower chamber. The lower chamber receives no fresh sewage directly, but is provided with gas vents and with means for drawing digested sludge from near the bottom.

Primary Settling.—The first settling tank through which sewage is passed in a treatment works.

Secondary.—A tank following a trickling filter or activated sludge aeration chamber.

Sedimentation.—A tank or basin. in which water, sewage, or other liquid containing settleable solids, is retained for a sufficient time, and in which the velocity of flow is sufficiently low, to remove by gravity a part of the suspended matter. Usually, in sewage treatment, the detention period is short enough to avoid anaerobic decomposition. Also termed Settling or Subsidence Tank.

Septic.—A single-story settling tank in which the settled sludge is in immediate contact with the sewage flowing through the tank, while the organic solids are decomposed by anaerobic bacterial action.

Sludge-Digestion--See Digester.

Thickener, Sludge.—A type of sedimentation tank in which the sludge is permitted to settle, usually equipped with scrapers traveling along the bottom of the tank which push the settled sludge to a sump, from which it is removed by gravity or by pumping.

Treatment.—Any definite process for modifying the state of matter.

Preliminary.—The conditioning of an industrial waste at its source prior 'to discharge, to remove or to neutralize substances injurious to sewers and treatment processes or to effect a partial reduction in load on the treatment process. In the treatment process, unit operations which prepare the liquor for subsequent major operations.

Primary.—The first major (sometimes the only) treatment in a sewage treatment works, usually sedimentation. The removal of a high percentage of suspended matter but little or no colloidal and dissolved matter.

Secondary.—The treatment of sewage by biological methods after primary treatment by sedimentation.

Sewage.—Any artificial process to which sewage is subjected in order to remove or alter its objectional constituents and thus to render it less offensive or dangerous.

Trap, Flame.—A device containing a fine metal gauze placed in a gas pipe, which prevents a flame from traveling back in the pipe and causing an explosion. See Arrester, Flame.

V

Venturi Meter.—A meter for measuring flow of water or other fluid through closed conduits or pipes, consisting of a Venturi tube and one of several proprietary forms of flow registering devices. The device was developed as a measuring device and patented by Clemens Herschel.

W

Waste Stabilization Pond.—Any pond, natural or artificial, receiving raw or partially treated sewage or waste, in which stabilization occurs due to sunlight, air, and microorganisms.

Water, Potable.—Water which does not contain objectionable pollution, contamination, minerals, or infection, and is considered satisfactory for domestic consumption.

Weir.—A dam with an edge or notch, sometimes arranged for measuring liquid flow.

Effluent —A weir at the outflow end of a sedimentation basin or other hydraulic structure.

Influent —A weir at the inflow end of a sedimentation basin.

Rectangular.—A weir whose notch is rectangular in shape.

Triangular.—A weir whose notch is triangular in shape, usually used to measure very small flows. Also called a V-notch.

Peripheral.—The outlet weir in a circular settling tank, extending around the inside of its circumference and over which the effluent discharges.

Rate.—See Loading, Weir.

Z

Zooglea.—A jelly-like matrix developed by bacteria, associated with growths in oxidizing beds.

Made in United States
North Haven, CT
19 May 2022

19321494R00083